Justice Takes a Recess

Justice Takes a Recess

Judicial Recess Appointments from George Washington to George W. Bush

SCOTT E. GRAVES AND ROBERT M. HOWARD

LEXINGTON BOOKS

A division of
ROWMAN & LITTLEFIELD PUBLISHERS, INC.
Lanham • Boulder • New York • Toronto • Plymouth, UK

LEXINGTON BOOKS

A division of Rowman & Littlefield Publishers, Inc.
A wholly owned subsidary of The Rowman & Littlefield Publishing Group, Inc.
4501 Forbes Boulevard, Suite 200
Lanham, MD 20706

Estover Road
Plymouth PL6 7PY
United Kingdom

British Library Cataloguing in Publication Information Available

Library of Congress Cataloging-in-Publication Data

Graves, Scott E., 1971–
  Justice takes a recess : judicial recess appointments from George Washington to George
W. Bush / Scott E. Graves and Robert M. Howard.
     p. cm.
  Includes bibliographical references and index.
  ISBN 978-0-7391-2661-5 (cloth : alk. paper)
  ISBN 978-0-7391-3819-9 (electronic)
  1. Judges—Selection and appointment—United States. I. Howard, Robert M., 1956– II.
Title.
  KF8776.G666 2009
  347.73'14—dc22   2009004795

Printed in the United States of America

♾™ The paper used in this publication meets the minimum requirements of American
National Standard for Information Sciences—Permanence of Paper for Printed Library
Materials, ANSI/NISO Z39.48–1992.

Dedications

Scott E. Graves:

To my father, Thomas M. Graves, Jr., my mother, Betty G. Graves, and my brother, Michael Graves

Robert M. Howard:

To my parents, Amy and Bernie Howard

Contents

Acknowledgements

Acknowledging the assistance of others is an exercise in balancing hazards. One risks omitting someone whose support, provided perhaps early in the project, was indispensible to the endeavor, but is overlooked in the reckoning. On the other hand, those mentioned stand in jeopardy of being implicated in a crime they didn't commit. Nevertheless, we owe a debt to many scholars who provided feedback on various parts and incarnations of the work in this book at conferences. In that regard, we would like to thank Rich Pacelle, Bradley Hays, Kevin McMahon, David Crocker, and Robert Spitzer.

We are particularly obliged to Pam Corley, for her contributions to Chapter 4.

Throughout the process of developing these materials into the book and preparing it for publication, we have been delighted to find the editors and staff with whom we've worked at Lexington and Rowman & Littlefield to be friendly, helpful, and capable. We would especially like to thank acquisitions editor Joseph C. Parry, editorial assistants Jana M. Wilson and Anna Miars, and assistant editor Ashley Baird.

For able research and other assistance, we'd like to thank Shenita Brazelton, Carol Walker, and Aimee Wickman.

Bob Howard would like to thank his family. To my children, Courtney and Jordan thank you for being wonderful, loving and always challenging. I am sorry that I made you Met fans, but blame Papa. To Dave, thank you for letting me adopt and support a Senator who is not from my home state. I thank my parents, Amy and Bernie Howard for all their sacrifice, love and devotion. I want to thank my late grandparents, Ivan and Rachel Skura and William and Anna Horowitz. You all let me grow up in an extended family atmosphere of love, support and really good food. I took this for granted and only many years later do I realize how lucky I was. Finally to Taryn, the love of my life and my best friend for all these years, with you "all losses are restored and sorrows end."

Scott Graves would like to thank his colleagues at Georgia State University for all of their insight and patience while this book was taking shape. During many conversations in halls and offices, knowingly or not, you helped me to think about the issues and implications of this work. In that spirit, I'd like to thank Rich Engstrom, Charles Hankla, Jeff Lazarus, Jason Reifler, and Amy Steigerwalt.

Chapter One

Of Time and the Constitution

Introduction

On April 9, 2003, President George W. Bush nominated William H. Pryor, Jr. to the United States Court of Appeals for the Eleventh Circuit. His confirmation stalled in the Senate when interest groups objected to his views on various matters. With the nomination languishing in the United States Senate, Congress adjourned for twelve days in mid-February, 2004, taking advantage of the Presidents' Day holiday weekend. During the congressional recess period, President Bush used his recess appointment power to install Pryor as judge, thus bypassing the confirmation process in the U.S. Senate. Pryor then resigned his position as attorney general for the state of Alabama and took his judicial oath for a term lasting until the end of 2006 when the next Congress begins.

The Senate eventually confirmed Pryor as a judge. However, before his confirmation, plaintiffs challenged the authority of the president to make this type of recess appointment. In *Evans v. Stephens,* 387 F.3d.1220 (2004), a divided *en banc* Eleventh Circuit rejected the plaintiffs' contentions and, with majority and dissenters differing on the plain meaning of the United States Constitution, upheld the appointment of their colleague, Judge Pryor.

The case sparked a vigorous debate within the court, with both sides offering similar theories of constitutional interpretation. Writing for the majority, Chief Judge J.L. Edmondson relied on text, intent, historical practice, and precedent to support the constitutionality of the appointment. He noted that the Constitution specifically says that "The President shall have Power to fill up all Vacancies that may happen during the Recess of the Senate, by granting Commissions which shall expire at the End of their next Session," and that vacancies refer to "Judges of the Supreme Court, and all other Officers of the United States, whose Appointments are note herein otherwise provided for, and which shall be established by law." The plain meaning of this clause was that the president is allowed to make temporary recess appointments to these offices, including all Article III courts such as the United States Circuit Courts of Appeals, without Senate approval.

Moreover, the court held that the phrase "the Recess of the Senate" does not limit the president to intersession as opposed to intrasession recesses. There is no language referring to any minimum time in these clauses, and presidents have several times made appointments during intrasession recesses even shorter than that in which the Pryor appointment was made.

There were two dissents to Chief Judge Edmondson's majority opinion. The first, by Judge Rosemary Barkett, challenged the interpretations of the Recess Appointment Clause proffered by the majority, highlighting the difficulty of interpreting the text of a document that is more than two hundred years old. Judge Barkett challenged the majority's assertion that where the language is susceptible of different interpretations, the court should defer to historical practice and the preferences of the other branches of government. Barkett argued that the intent of the framers, as evidenced by Alexander Hamilton in the Federalist Papers and Justice Joseph Story's early nineteenth-century treatise, was that the purpose of the Recess Appointment power was to enable the President to fill vacancies when the Senate was not able to act on the appointments, so that the operations of government and the administration of justice could be furthered. Thus, the Recess Appointment power was meant only for intersession, not intrasession, recesses. Otherwise, Judge Barkett argued, there would be nothing to prevent the President from repeatedly circumventing the Senate's advice and consent role.

In another dissent, Judge Charles R. Wilson was concerned with the risk to public confidence. As Judge Pryor had participated in almost three hundred appeals and authored over forty published and non-published opinions, granting the motion would imply that Judge Pryor was not qualified to sit on these other matters because he was not properly appointed, but denying the motion might lead to a questioning of the motives of the judges in that the court was more concerned with protecting a colleague than advancing the administration of justice.

The case highlights the difficulty of recess appointments. The majority and the Barkett dissent differed on the interpretation of language, text, intent, historical practice, and even precedent, but of course as the majority noted, this was not the first case of a recess appointed judge, nor the first case to challenge such an appointment.

An earlier case, *United States v. Woodley* (726 F.2d 1328 (9th Cir. 1982) challenged the rulings of a recess appointment of Walter Heen by President Jimmy Carter to the U.S. District Court for the District of Hawaii. Judge Heen then presided over the trial and conviction of Janet Woodley on drug charges. The Ninth Circuit analyzed the inherent tension between the President's recess appointment power under Article II which gives the Executive the power to "fill up all Vacancies that may happen during the Recess of the Senate, by granting Commissions which shall expire at the End of their next Session" and the attributes of judicial independence incorporated into Article III. It held that "only those judges enjoying Article III protections may exercise the judicial power of the United States" and vacated the lower court decision. According to the court, "[a] judge receiving his commission under the Recess Appointment

2

Clause may be called upon to make politically charged decisions while his nomination awaits approval by popularly elected officials. Such a judge will scarcely be oblivious to the effect his decision may have on the vote of these officials" (726 F.2d 1328 p. 1330, 1982). When a recess appointee hears a case, he or she does not have a permanent appointment, and whether the appointee receives tenure is still contingent upon renomination by the President and confirmation by the Senate (Mayton 2004).

Although the Ninth Circuit then reheard the case *en banc* and reversed, this was not the first time the idea that unconfirmed judges might be subject to unacceptable political pressures was broached. President Eisenhower ended a fifty-one-year-old informal moratorium on appointing Supreme Court justices through the Recess Appointment Clause with the appointment of Earl Warren as chief justice in 1953. Following the appointment, Professor Henry Hart objected:

> Governor Warren cannot possibly have this independence if his every vote, indeed his every question from the bench, is subject to the possibility of inquiry in later committee hearings and floor debates to determine his fitness to continue in judicial office. . . . The point is not what Governor Warren and his friends will think about his disinterestedness but what defeated litigants will think (Mayton 2004, 537).

The Recess Appointments of William Jefferson Clinton and George W. Bush

Many of these concerns were highlighted with the twin recess appointments to the Federal Circuit Courts of Appeals by President George W. Bush (Bashman 2004). One was of the aforementioned William H. Pryor, who later was confirmed by the Senate. A slightly earlier recess appointment was that of Charles Pickering to the Fifth Circuit Court of Appeals (Lewis 2004). Pickering, a long time Federal District Court judge in Mississippi, was nominated by President Bush to the Circuit Court in 2002, and again in the new Congress that started in 2003. Pickering's nomination, like the nomination of Pryor, stalled in the Senate. Pickering's critics, in the Senate and elsewhere, were troubled with his lack of support for abortion rights. However, the most damaging allegation arose from his seeming indifference, if not hostility, to civil rights. Senators and other critics questioned Pickering's record in this all important issue area. They noted that he has been critical of the Voting Rights Act of 1965, had seemingly gone out of his way to reduce the sentence of a man convicted of burning a cross, and critics also pointed to a law review article he wrote more than forty years ago suggesting ways to amend Mississippi's law banning interracial marriages so that it would pass constitutional muster. While Pickering repudiated the article and supporters argued his strong record of racial conciliation and strong support from the African American community in Mississippi, these allegations provided enough ammunition for the Senate to fail to vote on his nomination (King 2004).

During this period, several conservative commentators urged President Bush to make greater use of the recess appointment power, both for judicial appointments and for other positions in the executive branch of government. For example, one proponent of the recess appointment power accused Senate Democrats of instituting a "left-biased ideological litmus test for judges" (Williams 2002), and noted the high number of judicial vacancies. This commentator went on to argue that given the ongoing war on terror, such absences constituted an emergency, and this type of emergency is precisely the reason the framers designed the recess appointments clause. Others noted how President Clinton had used the recess appointment power to overcome Republican Senate opposition and nominate Roger Gregory as the first African American to sit on the United States Court of Appeals for the Fourth Circuit (Harrison 2003).

Finally, President Bush used his recess power to appoint Pickering in January of 2004 to the Court and then one month later appointed William Pryor. The Pickering and Pryor appointments received both praise and criticism. Many of the critical comments came from Democratic members of the Senate. Conservative commentators, on the other hand, praised the appointment arguing that Pickering and Pryor had been the victims of vicious personal attacks and were well qualified to be appellate court judges (Harrison 2003). In fact, many conservative organizations and individuals urged President Bush to make many more recess appointments to the judiciary.

However, under a deal worked out with Democratic senators, President Bush agreed to forego future recess appointments in return for the Senate agreeing to ratify twenty-five out of thirty controversial judicial nominations pending in the Senate (ABA report 2007, York 2004). Eventually, of course, the Senate confirmed Pryor's appointment, as it earlier confirmed the appointment of Roger Gregory. Pickering, unlike Pryor, withdrew his nomination in December 2004 when it was clear the new Senate would still refuse his confirmation, thus ending his tenure on the Court. This deal appeared to confirm the notion that President Bush was playing judicial poker with a weak hand (York 2004). Because of filibuster rules that, in effect, mandated sixty votes for confirmation, the president was unable to obtain the necessary votes for his judicial nominations. This senatorial weakness then led to the frustration and ultimate use of the recess appointment power, but with the accord, Bush agreed to suspend further use of the power for judicial appointments.

The Recess Appointment Power: The Key Questions

President Bush's use of the recess appointment power for judicial candidates is neither novel nor new, although before the appointment of Roger Gregory by

President Clinton the last recess appointment was by President Jimmy Carter of Walter Heen in December 1980. As the *Evans* majority and several commentators noted, since the beginning of the republic presidents have made over three hundred recess appointments to the federal judiciary including fifteen to the United States Supreme Court. Some presidents were more active than others. For example, President Eisenhower used the recess power to nominate Earl Warren in 1953, William Brennan in 1956, and Potter Stewart in 1958 to the Supreme Court. President Kennedy made twenty-three judicial recess appointments on the same day. These presidents are not alone in using judicial recess power in the twentieth century, in addition to Eisenhower and Kennedy, Theodore Roosevelt, Harry Truman, and Calvin Coolidge also made extensive use of the recess power and almost every president before the twentieth century made judicial recess appointments.

While one could debate the propriety or constitutional justifications for the very concept of the recess appointment power, the use of the recess power for judicial appointments presents a very different set of questions and issues than the use of the recess power for executive and independent agency appointments. As one scholar notes, there is conflicting evidence as to whether or not the framers ever intended the recess appointments clause to apply to the judiciary (Turley 2004). While it is not our purpose here to debate the constitutional underpinnings of the power to make judicial recess appointments, it is not hard to argue the difficulties of these types of appointments.

The judiciary, unlike the executive branch of government, is a separate and distinct branch of government. Hence recess appointments to the judiciary are separate and distinct from recess appointments to the executive branch of government. These appointments raise concerns that are highlighted by Professor Hart and the dissents in the above referenced cases. Such appointments seem to contradict the very ingrained notions of judicial independence, separation of powers, and the delicate balancing of majoritarian institutions such as the Congress, the presidency, and an anti-majoritarian institution such as the federal court system. While we do not expect courts to bow to the will of majority, in practice they reflect public opinion because they represent a collective choice of the nation's elected officials, to wit, the president and the Congress.

Given these concerns one begins to wonder why presidents use this power for the judiciary. We start with the notion that presidents, like legislators, and even judges, are rational. That is, presidents are purposeful, goal-seeking actors. In economic terms they seek to increase their utility. In political terms they seek to increase their power and policy preferences. We assume that presidents want to increase their power at the expense of Congress and conversely that Congress seeks to increase its power at the expense of the president.

All else being equal Congress and the presidency are two branches that framers intended to check and balance the power of each other. The federal court system becomes one way for each branch to shift and move both power and policy preferences. This is not to say partisan politics and shared policy preferences do not play a role in institutional separation of powers schemes. Shared preferences and party often unite the large blocs of Congress and the president, and enable each to overcome institutional differences and blunt a drive for institutional power.

There is an obvious, albeit temporary, gain in policy preferences. A president is able to get a (presumably) ideologically compatible judge on the bench immediately issuing rulings that the president favors. Those in Congress who support the president's and the nominee's policy positions might support the use of a judicial recess appointment particularly where it appears a minority of the Senate using the institutional structure of the filibuster thwart the preferences of the majority.

However there are significant costs. The president does not make a lifetime appointment. Instead the appointment only lasts until the end of the current congressional session. Thus the policy gain might be lost in a relatively short span of time. Further, the use of such powers antagonizes many in Congress, perhaps even those who support the nomination. The recess appointment, without presence of some sort of an emergency, clearly intrudes on the constitutional prerogatives of the Senate. As one aforementioned story relates, President Bush had to agree to forego the use of the recess power in order to obtain consent for the Senate to move on many of his other judicial nominations. To some, this demonstrated the president's weakness. Rather than serving as a source of source of authority for a president lacking political strength, recess appointment of judges can actually thwart presidential initiatives and expose his vulnerability. The power to appoint judges unilaterally serves the president's utility better as a chip to be bargained away in exchange for legislative cooperation.

Given the consequences of such appointments to judicial independence, separation of powers, and the balance of presidential, executive, and judicial power, the use judicial recess appointments brings into question both age-old and modern questions of constitutional authority, intergovernmental relations, and inter-branch interaction. The purpose of this book is our attempt to analyze and answer some basic questions in reference to judicial recess appointment process.

Thus in this book we seek to answer several simple yet intriguing questions. We begin by examining appointments over time. We address questions of change in the use of the power as technology changes over time. For example, does the recess appointment power make any sense in the modern world, and has presidential use of the recess appointment power has changed over time? Clearly the use of the recess appointment power in the eighteenth and nineteenth centuries had obvious value. In eras of limited transportation and difficult communication the ability of the executive to keep the operations of government functioning had obvious practical value. Congress did not sit all year, and before the invention of the telegraph, the post was the primary means of communication. Transportation and communication depended upon the speed of a horse and rider. The modern era, however, brings instantaneous communication and rapid travel. Have these developments changed the nature and use of the recess power?

We also answer broad questions on the use of the power: why and under what circumstances do presidents use this recess appointment power? How successful are the presidents in appointing judges with similar policy preferences? How successful are these presidents in obtaining Senate confirmation for these initially recess appointed judges? We pay special attention to the modern era with our ability to use up to date and sophisticated measures of voting, ideology, and policy preferences.

We also pay attention to whether or not the independence of recess appointees is compromised. What does a recess appointment mean for the judges who hear and decide cases while recess appointees? Do recess appointees vote differently when they sit under the recess appointment than when they sit after confirmation? Do they pay more attention to Senate preferences or the preferences of the Senate? Are they likely to shy away from issuing opinions or joining in on controversial cases? Are they less likely to dissent or concur? Is the behavior of the recess appointee to the United States Supreme Court different from the behavior of the recess appointee to a lower court?

We argue that this examination of the recess appointment power and the answers to these questions about judicial recess appointments is both timely and important. The use of the recess power can potentially upset the carefully calculated separation of powers envisioned by the framers, shifting power away from one branch of government towards another. It has the potential to undermine judicial independence and undermining confidence in the ability of the judiciary to dispense fair and impartial justice.

Chapter Overview

We proceed with four chapters to help us analyze these questions and issues. The rest of the book proceeds as follows:

Chapter Two: An Historical Overview and Analysis of Judicial Recess Appointments

In this chapter we provide an historical overview of judicial recess appointees. We examine the incidences of judicial recess appointment in every Senate recess from 1789 to 2005. We find that there has been a change over time in the use of judicial recess appointments, namely that as efficiency justifications have declined over time for recess appointments, there has been a corresponding decline in the use of the recess power. However, we also discover that presidents are conditionally strategic in their use of the unilateral authority to appoint federal court judges during Senate recesses, but that the use of this power is cautious and spare, especially in the modern era. Perhaps most surprisingly, and contrary to conventional wisdom, we find that strong presidents, not weak presidents, are most likely to take advantage of the recess appointment power and use it appoint judges, confident that such appointments will be confirmed.

Chapter Three: The Supreme Court Recess Appointments and Voting

We argue that Supreme Court appointments and other judicial appointments are analytically distinct and that voting patterns for Supreme Court justices are simply not comparable to the voting patterns of Appellate Court or District judges. When a recess-appointed judge hears a case, the appointee's tenure is still contingent upon renomination by the president and confirmation by the Senate. This circumstance calls into question the independence of the judge. Do judicial recess appointees behave differently during the recess appointment than they do after receiving Senate confirmation? We compare the votes of three Supreme Court justices during their recess appointment tenure with a similar period following Senate confirmation. We find that the justices appear to have voted differently during the time they sat as recess appointees, taking into account the partisan make-up of the Senate. In addition, the justices were less likely to cast controversial votes and less likely to write discretionary opinions pre-confirmation. Thus, it appears that judicial recess appointments do threaten judicial independence.

Chapter Four: Appellate Court Recess Appointments and Voting

Continuing on with our examination of voting behavior, in this chapter, along with co-author Pamela Corley, we compare the votes of post-war Appellate Court justices who were initially recess appointed during their recess appointment tenure with a similar period following Senate confirmation We explore this issue through the lens of separation of powers and judicial choice by examining judicial recess appointees who have later been confirmed by the Senate to full time Article III judicial positions. Specifically we compare the votes of seven modern recess appointed Courts of Appeals judges during their temporary appointment tenure with a similar period following Senate confirmation. We find substantial differences in pre- and post- confirmation voting. Using both different types of statistical models, we find that these judges are much more likely to vote in a liberal direction following confirmation in civil liberties and civil rights cases and much more willing to vote in contrast to Senate preferences following confirmation.

Chapter Five: A Look at Modern Judicial Recess Appointments

Since the 1960s, presidents have been very reluctant to bypass the advice and consent function of the U.S. Senate in order to temporarily place judges in judicial vacancies despite the consistent rise in the federal caseload and complaints of significant delays in confirmation during the same period. However, three controversial recess appointments in recent years, one by Bill Clinton in the last days of his presidency and two by George W. Bush in the face of minority obstruction in the Senate, were the first such appointments in over a decade and revived the controversy surrounding them. Both the occurrence and the circumstances of these appointments suggest the beginning of a new, more assertive use of the recess appointment power by presidents in the increasingly politicized activity of staffing the federal courts. We consider the relative influence of presidential, congressional, and judicial factors, including the continued institutionalization of the presidency, changes in the organization and work of the Senate, bargaining between the president and Congress, and the composition and output of the federal courts, on the incidence and timing of recess appointments to vacant seats in the federal courts. Our findings address why the practice declined so precipitously in the 1960s and what led to the apparent end of its dormancy in recent years. We conclude with some predictions about the role that recess appointments may play in the ongoing struggle between branches over the shape of the judiciary.

Chapter Six: A Skeptical View of Judicial Recess Appointments

We argue that the Recess Appointment Clause, particularly as it pertains to the judiciary, is no longer either necessary or desirable. It is a constitutional clause whose time has passed, now ranking with other clauses that one scholar labels "constitutional stupidities." In an age of instant communication, swift travel, and a full-time, professional legislature there is no compelling reason for judicial recess appointments. In fact our results showing the strategic use of such appointments by strong presidents to shift judicial ideology combined with the lack of independence exhibited by judicial recess appointees show the potential harm the recess power can cause in the modern era.

Conclusion

It is not our purpose to argue whether or the recess appointment power was meant to encompass judicial recess appointments. Nor is it our purpose to argue whether or not the phrase "recess" encompasses a short term "intrasession" break, or a longer and more formal "intersession" stoppage. No doubt these are important and interesting questions. While we offer suggestions and some normative ideas in our concluding chapter, in general, large scale theoretical and normative questions of constitutional interpretation, permissible exercises of executive power and the proper relationship of the president, the courts, and Congress are beyond the scope of this book.

We are political scientists, and our purpose is to examine and answer the above questions through empirical analysis. While much of our analyses and examinations are data driven and use various statistical models, one does not have to be a political scientist or familiar with statistical methodology to understand our arguments and our findings. In each chapter we offer explanations of our methods and our findings for the general reader. To be sure, those with greater understanding of the methodologies employed herein and who want to examine our methods and findings in greater detail will find all relevant information.

Chapter Two

An Historical Overview and Analysis of Judicial Recess Appointments

Introduction

Article II section 2 of the United States Constitution establishes that the president nominates the justices of the Supreme Court as well as "all other Officers of the United States by and with the advice and consent of the Senate." While there has been significant debate as to the meaning of "advice and consent" clearly it encompasses the right of the Senate to approve presidential nominations by a majority vote of the legislative body. The reason for this is argued by Alexander Hamilton, who wrote that Senate approval "would be an excellent check upon a spirit of favoritism in the President and . . . prevent the appointment of unfit characters" (Rossiter 1961, 457).

Article II section 2 also gives the executive the power to "fill up all Vacancies that may happen during the Recess of the Senate, by granting Commissions which shall expire at the End of their next Session." The purpose of the Recess Appointment Clause is clear—it allows the executive to keep the operations of government running even when the Senate is not in session and thus is unable to confirm presidential appointees. However, this clause also appears to upset the pristine formulation (Pyser 2006) of separated powers by allowing the president to bypass the Senate and appoint judges without any oversight not to mention the lack of "advice and consent."

While many scholars (Buck et al. 2005; Cardozo Law School Symposium 2005) have considered the propriety or constitutionality of recess appointments to the federal judiciary, in this chapter we seek to answer the simple yet intriguing questions of why and under what circumstances presidents use this recess appointment power. Given that most recess appointees are usually confirmed, why avoid an initial vote in the Senate to appoint a judge just for the remainder of the Congressional session? How does such a clause function in an age of instantaneous communication and speedy travel? We also address the question of whether presidential use of the recess appointment power has changed over time in response to changes in the relationship and power of governmental branches as well as changes in the nature and circumstances of Senate recesses. To answer these questions we examine all incidences of judicial recess appointments from George Washington in 1789 to George W. Bush in 2004.

These are important questions because the use of the recess power, like other unilateral powers vested with the president, can upset the carefully calculated separation of powers envisioned by the framers. In particular the abuse of this power can result in presidential favoritism or judges deemed "unfit" by a majority of senators. Two scholars of judicial appointments noted in a recent book that President Clinton's recess appointment of Roger Gregory to the Court of Appeals for the Fourth Circuit was the first recess appointment to the Judiciary since the presidency of Jimmy Carter in 1980 (Epstein and Segal, 2005, p. 81). Unlike most other unilateral presidential powers, judicial recess appointments are one of the few areas of politics that affect all three branches of government. They can shift power over the third branch away from the Congress and toward the executive branch.

In the ensuing chapter we explore under what political and institutional circumstances a president is likely to make a judicial recess appointment. While conventional wisdom holds that a politically weak president, lacking support in the Senate, is more likely to use the recess power to avoid the necessity of Senate approval, we find to the contrary in the modern era. We argue that politically strong presidents are more likely than weaker presidents to make judicial recess appointments. In a Separation of Powers system the recess appointment power allows a president to move the judiciary ideologically closer to his preferences, but this opportunity carries risks that political support can relieve. To demonstrate this we assess the literature on judicial appointments and judicial recess appointments. Next we offer a brief review of previous scholarship of presidential power. Then we present our data, methodology, and results of our study. Finally we offer our conclusions and suggestions for future research.

Judicial Appointments

While there has been little examination by political scientists of judicial *recess* appointments, the nomination and confirmation process of the judiciary has received significant scholarly attention. As several recent and classic books on judicial appointments make clear, presidential appointments to the federal judiciary have always been a contentious process driven by political and ideological concerns, both at the Supreme Court (Abraham 1992; Yalof 1999; Epstein and Segal 2005) and for lower courts (Epstein and Segal 2005). Although there are other considerations such as geographical balance, racial, ethnic, and gender diversity, and senatorial courtesy, presidents have consistently used the appointment power to nominate judges who will rule in a manner ideologically consistent with the preferences of the nominating president (Abraham 1992; Yalof 1999; Segal, Timpone, and Howard 2000; Epstein and Segal 2005). Some prominent scholars argue that ideological and political considerations and politicization have particularly increased since the presidencies of Ronald Reagan and the first President George H.W. Bush (see, e.g., Goldman 1997).

An Historical Overview and
Analysis of Judicial Recess Appointments

Republican presidents overwhelmingly appoint Republican judges and Democratic presidents overwhelmingly appoint Democratic judges (Segal and Spaeth 1993), although at least for the Supreme Court, political party matters less than ideology (Epstein and Segal 2005). On the whole, presidents are remarkably successful in pushing through their nominees and in finding ideologically similar justices (Segal, Timpone, and Howard 2000), even if ideological concordance between judges and presidents varies from president to president, at least at the Supreme Court level. In short, a president seeks to increase his institutional power through the appointment process. In a Separation of Powers system an ideologically compatible judiciary is far more likely than not to support presidential preferences (see Yates and Whitford 1998).

In order to achieve the goal of moving the federal judiciary in the direction of his ideological preferences, presidents must make strategic choices for lower courts as well as at the Supreme Court level (Massie, Hansford, and Songer 2004; Moraski and Shipan 1999). The Senate's constitutional role of providing "advice and consent" to permanent third branch appointments requires the president to choose nominees who can garner sufficient votes for confirmation, either a majority under ordinary circumstances, or filibuster-proof supermajorities under extraordinary conditions of conflict between the executive branch and the Senate minority, as observed recently.

However, presidents care about more than just eventual confirmation. Swift confirmation is also important. Several scholars have shown that delay rather than outright rejection is a key consideration for the president and a tool for those opposed to the appointment in the "advice and consent" confirmation process (Shipan and Shannon 2003; Binder and Maltzman 2002; Martinek, Kemper, and Van Winkle 2002; Nixon 2001). Delay is the great strategy of individual senators opposing the nominee (Bell 2002). Holding up the appointment can serve several goals for those opposing the nomination. A sufficiently significant enough delay can destroy the nomination or leave the president exposed as weak (Shipan and Shannon 2003; Nixon 2001). This can obstruct the president's other legislative priorities. In addition, delay can hinder and deter the president from achieving policy goals by delaying the appointment of likeminded ideologically compatible justices. Scholars have found that delay appears likely in times of divided government and also in times of ideological polarization within the Senate and between the Senate and the president (McCarty and Razaghian 1999; Bell 2002; Shipan and Shannon 2003).

Nevertheless, appointments to the judiciary, unlike the executive branch, can long outlast an individual presidency. The value of avoiding delay is unlikely to be great enough to offset the cost of failing to permanently seat a federal judge. Judicial recess appointments, therefore, call for careful considerations if they are to be used strategically. If the Senate and the president are each seeking greater institutional power, judicial nominations become a key battleground in that process. Greater ideological compatibility between the courts and either branch of government gives the executive or the legislature a key ally in moving policy preferences into public policy.

Recess Appointments

Although judicial recess appointment has fallen into disuse in recent years (Buck et al. 2004) a few recent appointments such as those of Roger Gregory, William H. Pryor, Jr., and Charles Pickering have highlighted the practice and led to both public interest (Hurt 2004) and scholarly analysis (Cardozo Law School Symposium 2005). The recess appointment of William H. Pryor, Jr. by President George W. Bush resulted in a court challenge of the constitutionality of recess appointment to Article III judicial seats. Pryor's confirmation stalled in the Senate when many interest groups objected to his views on various matters, leading to a filibuster by minority Democrats. With the nomination languishing in the United States Senate, Congress adjourned for twelve days in mid-February, 2004. During the congressional recess period President Bush used his recess appointment power to install Pryor as judge, bypassing the confirmation process in the U.S. Senate.

The Pryor appointment was challenged because the appointment was an intrasession recess appointment as opposed to an intersession recess appointment. The plaintiffs argued that a "recess" did not mean a relatively brief "intrasession" vacation or other temporary adjournment but rather referred to a longer formal "intersession" break, when there would be a significant need for government continuity and the administration of justice that would be severely hampered waiting for Congress to return. Eventually, in *Evans v. Stephens* (2004), a divided *en banc* Eleventh Circuit rejected the plaintiffs' contentions and, with majority and dissenters differing on the plain meaning of the United States Constitution upheld the appointment of their colleague Judge Pryor. Following the decision, a bipartisan agreement then allowed Pryor's nomination to be put to a vote and he was confirmed to a permanent seat on the Eleventh Circuit after sitting more than a year by recess appointment.

Given the prominence of the Pryor appointment and another judicial recess appointment by President George W. Bush in January 2004 of Charles W. Pickering Sr., whose nomination had previously been blocked twice in the Senate, scholars and jurists have recently devoted considerable attention to when and under what circumstances presidents should make recess appointments. However, there is nothing new about presidents using the recess appointment power to seat federal judges. George Washington appointed three judges to the Federal District Court during the recess of the First Congress. Fifteen Supreme Court justices have initially been seated through the recess appointment power, including Chief Justice Earl Warren and Associate Justices William Brennan and Potter Stewart, and presidents have made over three hundred recess appointments to the federal judiciary. Scholars have noted, however, the infrequent use of recess

Table 2.1: Recess Appointments and Confirmation Percentages							
President	Appts.	Conf.	%	President	Appts.	Conf.	%
George W. Bush (2001-present)	2	1	50	Chester Arthur (1881-85)	4	4	100
William J. Clinton (1993-2001)	1	1	100	James A. Garfield (1881)	2	2	100
George H.W. Bush (1989-93)	0	0	NA	Rutherford B. Hayes (1877-81)	3	3	100
Ronald Reagan (1981-89)	0	0	NA	Ulysses S. Grant (1869-77)	7	6	86
Jimmy Carter (1977-81)	1	0	0	Andrew Johnson (1865-69)	3	3	100
Gerald Ford (1974-77)	0	0	NA	Abraham Lincoln (1861-65)	9	8	89
Richard M. Nixon (1969-74)	0	0	NA	James Buchanan (1857-61)	1	1	100
Lyndon B. Johnson (1963-69)	4	3	75	Franklin Pierce (1853-57)	4	2	50
John F. Kennedy (1961-63)	25	25	100	Millard Fillmore (1850-53)	1	1	100
Dwight D. Eisenhower (1953-61)	27	26	96	Zachary Taylor (1849-50)	2	2	100
Harry S. Truman (1945-53)	39	33	85	James Polk (1845-49)	2	2	100
Franklin D. Roosevelt (1933-45)	15	13	87	John Tyler (1841-45)	0	0	NA
Herbert Hoover (1929-33)	9	8	89	William Henry Harrison (1841)	0	0	NA
Calvin Coolidge (1923-29)	25	22	88	Martin Van Buren (1837-41)	3	3	100
Warren G. Harding (1921-23)	5	5	100	Andrew Jackson (1829-37)	5	4	80
Woodrow Wilson (1913-21)	9	7	78	John Quincy Adams (1825-29)	6	5	83
William H. Taft (1909-13)	5	1	20	James Monroe (1817-25)	8	8	100
Theodore Roosevelt (1901-09)	30	26	87	James Madison (1809-17)	1	1	100
William McKinley (1897-1901)	11	9	82	Thomas Jefferson (1801-09)	8	7	88
Grover Cleveland (1893-97)	7	6	86	John Adams (1797-1801)	3	3	100
Benjamin Harrison (1889-93)	7	7	100	George Washington (1789-97)	9	8	89
Grover Cleveland (1885-89)	5	5	100	**Totals**	308	271	88

appointments to Article III judicial seats since President Kennedy. Judicial recess appointments are not innovative, untraditional uses of the president's constitutional authority, but they are controversial and, within the context of modern congressional-executive relations, problematic.

Table 2.1 provides a list of all judicial recess appointments made by the presidents of the United States from George Washington through George W. Bush. The data show that, with some exceptions, presidents are remarkably successful in having their judicial recess appointments confirmed by the Senate. Of the 308 recess appointments in Table 2.1, 271, or 88 percent, were later confirmed to full terms as federal judges. With the exception of John Tyler and William Henry Harrison (who died in office after only thirty days) all presidents in the eighteenth and nineteenth century used the appointment power including George Washington who made nine recess appointments.[1] The middle part of the twentieth century saw significant use, but its practice substantially declined from the presidency of Lyndon Johnson to the present with the recent exception of a few prominent, but controversial appointments described above.

Uses of the recess appointment power in recent decades have triggered substantial debate about the propriety and wisdom of the exercise of the recess appointment power. Following President Eisenhower's third placement of a Supreme Court justice during a recess, the Senate passed a resolution (S. Res. 334) opposing the practice. The resolution stated that recess appointments to the Supreme Court should be used only "under unusual and urgent circumstances" and the corresponding report from the Judiciary Committee asserted that such appointments obstructed the Senate's "solemn constitutional task" of providing advice and consent.[2] Despite the institutional prerogatives asserted, however, the resolution passed on a primarily partisan vote, forty-eight to thirty-seven (Fisher 2005).

More recently, recess appointments have become the focus of further contention and negotiation between presidents and the Senate. Following several non-judicial uses of the recess appointment by President Ronald Reagan, including one to the independent Federal Reserve Board of Governors, then-Senate Minority Leader Robert Byrd placed a hold on seventy other pending nominations, "touching virtually every area of the executive branch," according to the White House, as well as including federal judges (Fisher 2001, 11). Reagan's standoff with Byrd ended with the development of procedures for recess appointments, including notice prior to the beginning of the recess.[3] Violation of this agreement became one of the issues surrounding President Clinton's controversial recess appointment of Roger Gregory to a seat on the Fourth Circuit Court of Appeals. After the Democrats regained control of the Senate in the 1986 election, Senate Minority Leader Bob Dole (R-KS), a potential candidate for the presidency, raised the possibility of giving a recess appointment to Robert Bork in response to delay in Bork's confirmation hearings, a suggestion dismissed by a Senate Democrat as "playing politics" (Walsh 1987). No president has made such an appointment to the Supreme Court since the Senate's resolution discouraging it, but that episode and those during the Reagan and Clinton administrations demonstrate that although the Senate sees important institutional principles at stake in recess appointments, they are also perceived through the lens of partisan politics.

Of course, some presidents have used the recess appointment power more often than others. President Truman made the most appointments, 39, and confirmed 33 for a success rate of 87 percent. Theodore Roosevelt followed Truman with thirty appointments, twenty-six of whom were confirmed for an 87 percent success rate. Presidents Eisenhower (twenty-seven with twenty-six confirmed) and Kennedy (twenty-five, all confirmed) made extensive use of the recess appointment power and were very successful in having their appointments confirmed.

Several scholars (Carrier 1994; Cardozo Law School Symposium 2005; Pyser 2006) have noted that the recess appointment power was of obvious value in the eighteenth century when limited transportation and a part time Congress meant that the chief executive needed a mechanism to keep the operations of government functioning, including the judiciary. Congress used to adjourn for much longer periods of time, and it was technologically impossible to reconvene Congress in a short period of time. It was the very different nature of Congressional recesses that led to the challenge of Pryor's intrasession recess appointment. However, with the Eleventh Circuit decision upholding the intrasession recess of William H. Pryor and previous decisions upholding the constitutionality of judicial recess appointments, it is clear that whatever the normative desirability of such appointments federal courts have upheld the recess appointment power. The issue then becomes why and under what circumstances presidents will use this power.

Time and Presidential Power

In contrast to the shared authority of appointment laid out by the conventional process, the recess appointment power vests the president with the ability to act unilaterally, without the consent of and possibly contrary to the advice of the Senate. Like other unilateral powers possessed by the president, the recess appointment power can be conceived of as a strategic tool employed by the executive to act when the legislative process stands in the way of his goals. More than other unilateral powers, a recess appointment can alter the balance of power between all three branches of government. That is, recess appointments can serve as a way for presidents to influence the exercise of judicial power separate from, if not indifferent to, the power to persuade the legislature. Alternatively, presidential powers may be used as a complement to legislative action, or at least with care due to the prerogatives of Congress, rather than as a substitute for traditional inter-branch relations.

Recess Appointments and Executive Orders

Research on the use of executive orders has elaborated on these different conceptions of unilateral presidential power. Although some scholars have discovered evidence that executive orders are used strategically when legislative obstruction can be anticipated (Deering and Maltzman 1999; Mayer 1999), others have concluded that executive orders are used in coordination with successful legislative activity or in favorable political circumstances (Krause and Cohen 1997; Mayer 1999; Shull 1997). Also, several studies contend that developments entirely within the executive branch influence the use of executive orders (King and Ragsdale 1988; Krause and Cohen 2000). Marshall and Pacelle (2005) found that the production of executive orders responds differently to institutional and political circumstances across issue areas, while Krause and Cohen (2000) identified a shift in the effect of a variety of factors on executive orders across time periods. Specifically, they concluded that constraints from Congress had a stronger effect on the issuance of executive orders after the "institutionalized" presidency had developed fully. Earlier presidents' use of executive orders was driven more by intra-institutional concerns, opportunities for presidential action, rather than constraints.

From these findings on executive orders, we draw our two specific queries. First, do presidents use recess appointments in a strategic, perhaps confrontational fashion in order to achieve policy goals they would not be able to achieve through the conventional appointment process? Second, has the use of recess appointments changed over time as presidential power and the length and nature of Senate recesses changed?

On its face, a recess appointment to an Article III court allows the president to fill a vacancy with a favored candidate quickly, without the obstruction or rejection the confirmation process might produce. Such appointments are temporary, but an intrasession recess commission can last for nearly two years, if the recess falls early in the congressional session (Carrier 1994). This allows the president to appoint an ideologically compatible judge to serve on an Article III court producing rulings that the president favors for a significant period of time. Little quantitative research has been conducted on recess appointments, but one study (Corley 2003) finds that the president is more likely to recess appoint an independent commissioner when the president is ideologically distant from the Senate and when the president's approval ratings are low.[4]

Other considerations suggest that recess appointments may be used for reasons other than the advancement of purely political goals. As described above, when the Constitution was ratified and throughout the eighteenth century, the recess appointment power had clear justification due to the length of Senate recesses and the time-consuming nature of travel across the ever-expanding nation. Whittington and Carpenter note that the makeup of the executive branch predisposes the president to be motivated more by "efficiency, effectiveness, and national strength" compared to the legislature (2003, 498).

Also, as effective as a well-placed recess appointment to the federal judiciary could be, its immediate and long-term costs may outweigh or negate its short-term policy effectiveness. "When presidents have used temporary or recess appointments . . . to bypass the confirmation process," Gerhardt notes, "senators have invariably used their other powers, particularly oversight and appropriations, to put pressure on those choices" (2000, 174). Furthermore, the ability of a president to extend his influence beyond his terms of office by reshaping the federal judiciary through life-term appointments is not served, and may be frustrated, by the injudicious use of unilateral authority like the recess appointment power. Thus, the use of recess appointments may have changed as a consequence of temporal or institutional changes. Recent controversies over recess appointments, especially to fill vacancies in the judicial branch, have raised the lack of compelling traditional justification for these appointments such as the unavailability of Congress for extended periods. To take a preliminary look at the relationship between judicial recess appointment practice and recess length, Figure 2.1 presents a graph of both series. Examining the average length of Senate recesses over time, we see a dramatic and enduring decline beginning at around the 90th Congress in the late 1960s. This decline coincides with the recent drop in the incidence of recess appointments to the federal bench, suggesting that the latter trend may be in large part due to the diminished justification

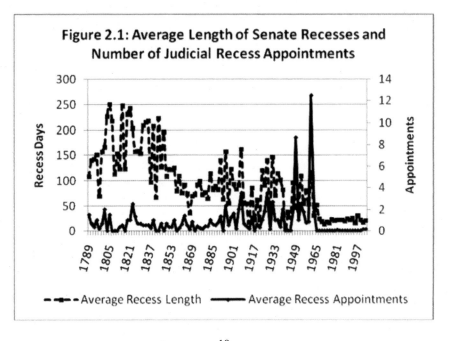

Figure 2.1: Average Length of Senate Recesses and Number of Judicial Recess Appointments

for such appointments. We should expect that recess appointments will be less common in the absence of reasons for them. Moreover, those that do occur under such circumstances, we anticipate, may spring from more political or policy-based motives. Following Krause and Cohen (2000), we also suspect that changes in the nature of presidential power over time could have altered the relationships between various factors and the incidence of recess appointments.

The Effect of Time

The effect of time on the use of presidential powers can be conceived of in a variety of ways. Skowronek (1993), for example, distinguishes secular and political time. Secular time is related to the expansion of resources and responsibility. Skowronek then follows this time through four distinct presidential eras of the nation's history and shows how the accumulation of power is dependent upon the uses of power appropriate to the particular era–patrician, partisan, pluralist, or plebiscitary.

Lewis and Strine (1996) describe four different conceptions of "presidential time": secular, regime, modern, and political time. "Secular presidential time" as they describe it proposes that presidents have benefited from a monotonic increase in power since the beginning of the Republic. A "regime time" approach divides presidencies into a number of time periods. "Modern" presidential time contrasts the presidency before and after a transformation period. Lewis and Strine demarcate the beginning of the modern era with FDR.

Lewis and Strine analyze secular and regime time by "looking for broad trends in veto use over the 1890-1994 period" (690). The authors expected that the effect of a secular increase in presidential power over time will result in a steady decline in vetoes, but found no such pattern. Likewise, we observe no indication that recess appointments to the courts have either monotonically increased, or decreased, which would be the case if presidential power to reshape the judiciary through conventional appointments increased consistently.

Turning to regime time, Lewis and Strine admit that "[n]o explicit hypotheses exist to explain how presidents within regime cycles will use power" (1996, 687). Nevertheless, they sketch some expectations about veto use by various presidents at different points within regime time and test them by examining the differences in veto production across presidents from 1890 to 1994. They acknowledge that including presidents whose regime positions are uncertain or who seem atypical of their regime positions would "leave us with much murkier results" (1996, 698). The authors noted that presidents "may share similar positions in the regime cycle but their positions are fundamentally different because of the changes that have occurred in the presidency between the tenures of the two presidents" (1996, 697).

Conducting an event count analysis, Lewis and Strine find that use of the veto corresponds to their expectations of the modern/early conception of presidential power, but not with their predictions about political time. Of particular interest, they find a substantial shift in presidential power with the beginning of the modern presidency, especially with regard to the president's legislative activity. Presidential power in modern time is not merely different in magnitude from the pre-FDR era; the nature of its use is different.

We note that the veto is similar to the recess appointment power in some ways—both are reactive to opportunity—but different in several important respects. A presidential veto is an answer to congressional action, typically a hostile one, while recess appointments are often a response to Senate inaction. Furthermore, a recess appointment stresses the president's proposal advantages in a way vetoes do not. Because the president usually wants the Senate to confirm the person he has temporarily seated, the recess appointment can be thought of as an invitation rather than a rebuff.

Recess appointments share several qualities with the president's authority to issue executive orders, discussed above. Many scholars have observed that executive orders tend to proliferate with increases in the president's legislative strength and success (Krause and Cohen 1997; Mayer 1999). Not only can legislative support facilitate or increase the value of executive orders, using them as an end run around Congress carries substantial risk. As Cooper notes, "Clinton, Reagan, Carter, Nixon, and Johnson, among recent presidents, encountered significant difficulties . . . by challenging the legislature using executive orders" (2002, 71).

In order to get an initial idea of the coincidence of recess appointments per Senate recess and executive orders across time, Figure 2.2 plots these two series. Although not as overt as the relationship in Figure 2.1, the production of executive orders per presidential term appears to follow a distinct, non-monotonic secular trend, rising and falling with the advent of the administrative presidency. A vertical line marks the 72nd Congress, the final Congress before the Roosevelt era. In contrast to the stylized account of an ever-increasing administrative state and executive power, the figure indicates that after slight but consistent growth, executive orders rose abruptly preceding FDR, spiking during the Great Depression and WWII. After Roosevelt's abbreviated last term and demobilization under Truman, the rate of executive order production appears to have settled back to a level not inconsistent with pre-twentieth century trends, but displaying considerably more volatility. The dispersion of recess appointments during and after FDR's presidency is, if anything, slightly sparer than before.

For the purposes of this study, we take note of Lewis and Strine's identification of a shift in the use of presidential power coinciding with the Roosevelt administration and the advent of the "modern" presidency. We expect that the use of judicial recess appointments in the "modern" presidential era will differ from the earlier era. Changes in the nature of presidential power, combined with

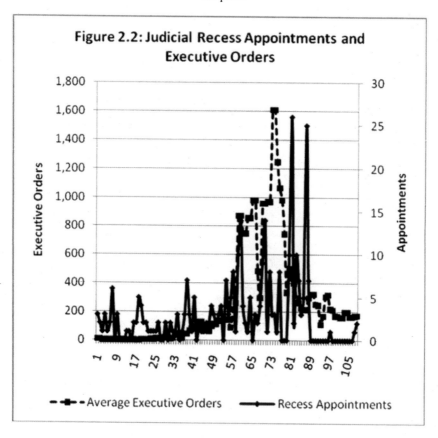

Figure 2.2: Judicial Recess Appointments and Executive Orders

— ■ —Average Executive Orders ——•——Recess Appointments

the decline in previous, efficiency-based justifications for recess appointments, suggest that presidents in the modern era should be more careful with their use of this power and sensitive to the political costs of short-circuiting the traditional path of appointment through the Senate. Therefore, we believe that modern presidents will respond differently to the circumstances surrounding the opportunity to make a recess appointment than those in the earlier era.

Data, Methods, and Model

Our study examines incidences of recess appointments in every Senate recess from 1789 to 2004 stretching from George Washington to the end of George W. Bush's first term.[5] Toward that end we collected data on these recesses, such as the length in days of each recess, and whether or not the recess was intersession, as identified by the *Congressional Directory*. From data collected by the Federalist Society for Law and Public Policy, we identified the number of recess appointments made to Article III courts in each of the recesses (Buck et al. 2004).[6]

Guided by theory and previous studies, we expect that several factors will affect the use of recess appointments to Article III courts. Presidents and the Senate have long contested the meaning of a "recess" for the purposes of Article II, Sec. 2. Even though the power of presidents to make such appointments during an intersession recess, following the *sine die* adjournment of a session of Congress, has not been contested, appointments during intrasession recesses have been both controversial and rare. Thus, we coded a variable for each recess identifying whether or not it was intrasession and anticipate that appointments during such recesses will be comparatively uncommon. We also calculated the length of the Senate recess, hypothesizing that longer recesses are more likely to produce lengthy vacancies that could impair the function of the judicial branch and prompt a recess appointment.

Despite the conventional wisdom that presidents rely on unilateral powers, especially the recess appointment power, when they are politically weak in the legislature, we are persuaded by the findings of the executive orders literature and expect that the strength of the president's party in the Senate will make recess appointments more, rather than less, likely. Our explanation, however, is slightly different. Rather than using executive orders to build upon legislative successes, we believe that recess appointments are politically safer for the president when he has a strong partisan majority in the Senate to protect his legislative agenda from obstruction. This relationship should be especially strong in the "modern era," after the expectation of executive involvement with the legislature strengthened. We measured the strength of the president's party in the Senate during each recess in the dataset as the proportion of seats held at that time.

Another factor that we believe will influence the use of recess appointments is the value of the appointment itself. Although there are several ways to measure the value of a judicial appointment, one that lends itself particularly well to our aggregate data and the temporal nature of the recess appointment is the length of time the appointee will sit. The commissions issued to recess appointees expire at the end of the next session of Congress, which, in the case of an intersession recess, is the end of the next convening session. For intrasession recesses, however, the commission does not expire until the end of the following session, rather than the end of the session within which the recess falls. To capture these effects, we measure the length in days from the end of each recess until the end of the following session, taking into account the difference between inter- and intrasession recesses. We expect that the longer that period of time is, the longer the temporary commission will last, the greater the likelihood of a recess appointment.

The presidency literature suggests that presidential powers, even discretionary powers like executive orders, are used with sensitivity to the Congress and the agenda of the president. We hypothesize that recess appointments to the judiciary will be related to the use of the other major discretionary, self-initiated presidential power, the executive order, but in a time-bound way. Prior to the modern era, before the institutionalization of the executive office, we anticipate that executive orders will be positively related to recess appointments, as both are driven more by opportunity and intra-branch concern for efficiency, the "energetic" characteristics of the early presidency. A president who governs substantially by executive order is also more likely to use recess appointments.

In the modern era, however, efficiency concerns borne of legislative recess are less pressing while the expectation of executive involvement with the legislature has increased. As judicial recess appointments become more difficult to justify in traditional terms, opportunistic uses could jeopardize the president's relationship with the Senate, delaying or derailing other appointments or legislative initiatives. Therefore, we hypothesize that modern presidents will use recess appointments, for want of a better word, judiciously, balancing their executive lawmaking authority and unilateral appointment power to avoid too many confrontations with Congress. Under such circumstances, we expect a negative relationship between executive orders and recess appointments. To test that relationship, we collected the number of executive orders issued by the presidential administration in which each recess fell.

We have differing sets of hypotheses for various factors across the early/modern time divide. Therefore, we included a variable to indicate whether or not the recess occurred before or after the beginning of the first FDR presidency. We also produced multiplicative interactions of several variables with the indicator for the modern presidency, including the president's party strength in the Senate, the length of time until the end of the next session, and the number of executive orders. We also include several variables as controls. We collected the number of authorized judicial seats at the time of each recess to account for the varying number of opportunities present over time. Also, to test the conventional account of recess appointments, we coded a variable to indicate whether the Senate and president were held by different parties at the time of the recess. If recess appointments are used primarily to circumvent Senate intransigence, we should expect that the likelihood of observing recess appointments should increase when the branches are so divided.

In order to control for the monotonic increase in the number of federal circuit court judicial seats over time, increasing the number of positions to be filled, we include the natural log of the number of authorized Article III judges. The anticipated direction of its effect is positive; as the number of judicial positions increases, the number of opportunities to make recess appointments will rise. In event count analysis, a variable of this nature is often referred to as an "exposure" effect (Cameron and Trivedi 1998, 81). Our data are summarized in Table 2.2. The expected effects for the Zero-Inflation Equation reflect the expected relationship between changes in the variable and the likelihood of being in the "zero only" state, so positive parameters indicate a direct relationship be-

Variable	"Early" Presidency (N = 285) Mean (SD)	"Modern" Presidency (N = 340) Mean (SD)	Complete Data (N = 625) Mean (SD)	Expected Direction of Effect	
				Outcome Equation	Zero-inflation Equation
Recess Appointments	0.702 (1.567)	0.338 (1.899)	0.502 (1.762)	Outcome Equation	Zero-inflation Equation
Intrasession Recess	0.253 (0.435)	0.776 (0.417)	0.538 (0.499)	−	+
Length of Recess (nl[days])	3.622 (1.752)	2.851 (0.925)	3.202 (1.418)	+	−
Senate Strength (proportion)	0.570 (0.143)	0.512 (0.084)	0.538 (0.118)	+	NA
Divided Government	0.218 (0.413)	0.479 (0.500)	0.36 (0.480)	NA	−
Length of Appointment (nl[days])	4.368 (1.223)	6.074 (0.459)	5.404 (1.183)	+	NA
Executive Orders (100s)	2.519 (3.487)	2.642 (2.558)	2.637 (3.021)	+	−
Exposure (nl[Article III seats])	4.26 (0.656)	6.403 (0.388)	5.418 (1.185)	+	NA
Modern Presidency (Post 1932)			0.544 (0.498)	−	+
Modern × Senate Strength			0.278 (0.262)	+	NA
Modern × Length of Appointment			3.304 (3.047)	+	NA
Modern × Executive Orders (100s)			1.488 (2.333)	−	−

Table 2.2: Descriptive Statistics and Expected Relationships, Senate Recesses

tween the variable and observing no recess appointments during the recess in question. One of the first things to note about the data is the distribution of the dependent variable. The number of recess appointments made in a given recess is a discrete, non-negative outcome that ranges, in practice, from zero to twenty-three. The mean, however, is less than .5 for the entire dataset and the standard deviation is below two. Table 2.3 presents the frequency distribution of the variable. The distribution is dominated by zeros; over 80 percent of recesses have no recess appointments. The remaining distribution of non-zero observations also skews low, with 97.5 percent of the cumulative distribution (and over 80 percent of the non-zero observations) at four recess appointments or below.

The standard method for discrete, non-zero count outcomes, the Poisson regression model common to veto and executive order studies, makes the restrictive assumption of equidisperion. That is, that the conditional mean and variance of the dependent variable are equal (Cameron and Triveldi 1998, 21). In fact, the observed variance of our outcome is more than six times its mean. Although excess zeros will cause overdispersion and overdispersion can result in excess zeros, the distribution of the dependent variable suggests that both problems exist independently. Even excluding the zero counts from our data, the variance

Table 2.3: Frequency Distribution of Recess Appointments by Recess, 1789-2005

Recess Appointments	Frequency	Percent	Cumulative Percentage
0	515	82.40	82.40
1	39	6.24	88.64
2	35	5.60	94.24
3	14	2.24	96.48
4	6	0.96	97.44
5	3	0.48	97.92
6	5	0.80	98.72
7	3	0.48	99.20
9	2	0.32	99.52
11	1	0.16	99.68
22	1	0.16	99.84
23	1	0.16	100.0

of the dependent variable is nearly four times the mean of the remaining observations.

To address both of these problems, we estimate a zero-inflated negative binomial regression model.[7] Under our specification, the observed data is the result of a process that produces zero recess appointments with some probability, parameterized with covariates as a logit equation, and another process that produces a non-negative count of recess appointments following a negative binomial distribution.

Results and Analysis

The results of the zero-inflated negative binomial model are presented in Table 2.4. The standard errors for the ZINB model are robust, clustered on the president. A likelihood ratio test of the variance factor α rejects the null of equidispersion and an adaptation of the Normally-distributed Vuong test for non-nested models applied to the zero-inflation equation rejects the null of no significant zero-inflation at an alpha of .001. Many of the hypothesized effects receive support as well. Intrasession recesses are significantly related to a decrease in the number of recess appointments observed and directly related to the production of zero-count recesses.[8] The length of Senate recesses[9] likewise has a consistent effect on recess appointments, decreasing the likelihood of observing a zero-state and increasing the conditional mean of the outcome.

The potential value of the recess appointment is significant and positive. This means that presidents are likely to produce more recess appointments as the length of time that appointees will sit grows. Interestingly, although the coefficient for the interaction of this variable with the modern era is positive, it is not statistically different from zero. It appears that this strategic use of recess

Table 2.4: Zero-Inflated Negative Binomial Model of Recess Appointments per Senate Recess, 1789-2004

Outcome (Event Count)	Coefficient (SE)	Z-score	Incidence Rate Ratio
Intrasession Recess	-.928 (.226)	-4.11***	.40
Length of Recess (nl[days])	.995 (.219)	4.54***	2.70
Senate Strength (proportion)	-.377 (.717)	-0.53	
Appointment Length (nl[days])	.355 (.193)	1.84*	1.43
Executive Orders (100s)	.095 (.041)	2.33**	1.10
Modern Presidency (Post 1932)	-4.489 (3.278)	-1.37	
Modern × Senate Strength	5.515 (2.135)	2.58**	248.37
Modern × Length of Appointment	.601 (.558)	1.08	
Modern × Executive Orders (100s)	-.260 (.048)	-5.43***	.77
Exposure (nl[Article III judicial seats])	.314 (.202)	1.55	
Constant	-7.941		
α	.409		
Likelihood-ratio test of α = 0 $\chi^2(1) = 41.02$***			

Zero-inflation (Logit)	Coefficient (SE)	Z-score	Odds Ratio
Intrasession Recess	1.544 (.575)	2.69**	4.68
Length of Recess (nl[days])	-1.176 (.487)	-2.42**	.31
Divided Government	-.556 (.786)	-0.71	
Executive Orders (100s)	-.073 (.158)	-0.46	
Modern Presidency (Post 1932)	4.955 (2.383)	2.08*	141.94
Modern × Executive Orders (100s)	-1.336 (.544)	-2.46**	.26
Constant	4.304		
Vuong test of zero-inflation Z = 3.50***			

Likelihood ratio test (16 df) = 327.016***
N = 625

*** / ** / * = significant at p < .001 / p < .01 / p < .05, one-tailed tests

appointments is invariant across time periods. The coefficient for the strength of the president's party in the Senate is not significantly different from zero, but interacting it with the modern era dummy produces a significant and positive coefficient. This indicates that during the modern era, a rise in the proportion of the Senate controlled by the president's party results in an increase in the expected number of recess appointments.

The estimated relationship of executive orders to recess appointments is complicated. The constituent term is unrelated to the probability of being in the zero-state, but its coefficient is positive in the negative binomial equation. Thus, an increase in the number of executive orders issued during the current administration of the president in office during the recess increases the expected number of recess appointments. However, the interaction terms of executive orders with the modern era are significant in both equations. Modern presidents who produce more executive orders are significantly more likely not to make a recess appointment.

Several other results are worth noting. Cursory review of the summary statistics reveals that judicial recess appointments have been less common during the modern era, both in absolute numbers and per recess. The dummy variable for the modern era produces a significant and positive coefficient, indicating that recesses in the modern era are more likely, all else equal, to be in the zero-appointment state. The divided government variable, entered in the zero-inflation equation, is negative, as expected if divided government makes the use of the recess appointment power more likely, but not statistically distinguishable from zero. The variable controlling for exposure, the natural log of the number of Article III judgeships authorized at the time of the recess, is positive but insignificant in the negative binomial equation. This result is not entirely unexpected, as growth in the size of the federal judiciary has coincided with a decline in recess appointments. We conclude from this finding, however, that "opportunities" for recess appointments should be understood not in terms of the number of potential vacancies to be filled, but in terms of the conditions favoring such an appointment, which have become rarer even as the federal bench expanded.

Because event count models are nonlinear, we present transformations of the estimated coefficients in the fourth column of Table 2.4. For the negative binomial equation, we include the incidence rate ratio for each significant coefficient, which reflects the factor change in the expected count for a unit change in the variable in question, other variables held constant. An intrasession recess has a substantial impact on the expected count of recess appointments, reducing it by more than 60 percent. A unit change[10] in the length of the recess is estimated to have the effect of increasing the expected count by more than a factor of 2.7. The standard deviation of the variable is greater than one, so an increase of one standard deviation has an even greater effect (4.1).

An increase in the length of the recess appointment itself produces a factor change of 1.43 on the expected outcome for one unit, but a standard deviation increase produces a 1.52 factor change. The incidence rate ratio of Senate strength in the modern era is 248.4, but since the variable never observes a unit change (which could happen only if the president's party increased its seat share in the Senate from zero to one hundred) a more useful comparison is the factor change for an increase in one standard deviation, which is 4.24.

Interpretation of the impact of executive orders is also complex. The incidence rate ratio of executive orders (measured in hundreds) is 1.10, a modest 10 percent increase in the expected count for a unit increase in executive orders, but during the modern era that effect is coupled with a .77 rate ratio, producing approximately a .85 rate ratio for the combined impact. The standard deviation of executive orders is greater than 3, and the factor change for an increase of one such deviation is 1.33, but again the effect is counteracted by a 6.25 factor change for recesses in the modern era.

Turning to the zero-inflation equation, Table 2.4 presents odds ratios, which have an interpretation similar to incidence rate ratios for count models. The odds ratio represents the change in the odds of a positive outcome (in this case, the likelihood that the recess is in the zero-state) for a unit increase in the variable. An intrasession recess is considerably more likely to be in a zero-only state, nearly 4.7 times as likely, as an intersession recess. An increase in the length of the recess, however, makes the zero-state less likely by a factor of .3 for a unit increase or by .19 for a change of one standard deviation. Recesses occurring in the modern era, most of which are intrasession and brief, are far more likely to be in the zero-state. All else equal, a recess is about 141 times as likely to produce zero recess appointments during or after the presidency of Franklin Roosevelt. Finally, a unit change in the number of executive orders in the modern era produces a factor change of .26, over a 70 percent decrease in the likelihood of being in the zero-state. A standard deviation increase carries a factor change of about .05, or a 95 percent decrease in the same likelihood.

Conclusions

The findings of this analysis echo many of the conclusions of other studies of presidential authority. We discover that presidents are conditionally strategic in their use of the unilateral authority to appoint federal court judges during Senate recesses, but that the use of this power is careful and spare, especially in the modern era. Our results conform to what we believe to be the canonical uses anticipated when the power was extended. As efficiency justifications have declined, so have incidences of recess appointments, and the length of Senate recess has a significant and substantial effect on recess appointments. The estimated relationship between the length of Senate recesses and the incidence of recess appointments bears out the striking connection visible in Figure 2.1 and suggests that the rarity of such appointments in recent decades is in part an ordinary function of a change in Senate business.

However, this is not the only story. We also uncover evidence of strategic and opportunistic presidential use of the recess appointment. The length of time an appointee will sit has a significant, positive impact, and active presidents, measured by the number of executive orders issued, are more likely to produce recess appointments, but albeit fewer in number. We identify a change in recess appointments unconnected to the developments in congressional sessions. Consistent with the advent of a modern institutionalized presidency that engages considerably with the legislature, but is consequently tied to a substantial legislative agenda, we find that recent presidents balance their exercise of unilateral powers and use strong partisan majorities to shield themselves from the consequences of dispensing with advice and consent. Recess appointments that appear to be made at the expense of political capital and attention to other domestic policy initiatives bear the hallmarks of political or policy-motivated action, rather than the efficiency-oriented use contemplated for recess appointments.

In that context, the recent recess appointments of President Bush are somewhat atypical, made as they were when the Republican Party held a bare majority in the Senate. The remarkable party discipline exercised by the GOP, which has also allowed him to veto merely one bill in over five years (as of October 2006), might help explain the anomaly. In contrast, the Justice Department's dismissal of eight U.S. attorneys to be replaced by never-expiring interim appointees without Senate oversight in late 2006 has, with Democrats now in control of Congress, prompted hearings in both Houses and the resignation of the Justice Department official personally responsible for the dismissals (Johnston 2007).

President Clinton's appointment of Roger Gregory, made when the Democrats were a minority in the Senate, was also atypical in these terms. Clinton's appointment was perhaps even more unusual because Gregory was eventually confirmed to a life appointment after renomination by his successor, although the Democrats had narrowly regained control of the Senate by that time. However, given that Clinton upset a long-standing understanding between the executive and legislative branches on recess appointments it is arguably a very strategic use of the recess appointment power and one that led to Gregory's confirmation.

Our results suggest that contemporary use of the recess appointment power to fill federal judicial seats should be greeted with skepticism. Republican Senators Trent Lott and James Inhofe spoke vehemently against Gregory's appointment and President George W. Bush's appointments were met with similar condemnation from Democratic Senators. Gregory and Pickering's recess appointments were both made intersession, abiding by the narrower understanding of the recess appointments clause favored by many senators and representing the shortest duration for recess commissions. However, Clinton appointed Gregory during a recess that lasted less than three weeks and Pickering's appointment was made during one of the longest Senate recesses in recent years, just over five weeks. Given their observed sensitivity to the length an appointee will sit and other indicators that modern presidents make recess appointments in an opportunistic fashion, combined with the legal and political controversy surrounding them, we believe that judicial recess appointments are unjustified.

The unavailability of data back to the beginning of the Republic make it impossible to include ideological distance measures between the president and Senate, approval scores, and other useful factors in our analysis. The difficulty of disaggregating appointment data over such a lengthy period also limits our analysis. Closer study of judicial recess appointments confined to the modern era could take into account these additional factors and possibly find other ways in which the exercise of unilateral presidential power has been complicated since the institutionalization of the American presidency.

Notes to Chapter 2

1. Controversies over judicial recess appointments are not an entirely new phenomenon. One of President Washington's recess appointments was of John Rutledge to Chief Justice of the United States, igniting a controversy, which, according to Curtis (1984, 1775-6) contributed to his rejection by the Senate.

2. 106 Cong. Rec. 12761 (1960); S. Rept. No. 1893, 86th Cong., 2nd Session 1-2 (1960).

3. Ironically, a requirement that the President notify the Senate before a recess in which he intends to make a recess appointment makes impossible an initial interpretation of Art II Sec 2, favored by proponents of strong legislative oversight, which limited the president to temporary appointments only to fill vacancies that come into being during a Senate recess (Fisher 2001).

4. However, the same study concludes that a nominee from a different party than the Senate majority is not more likely to be recess appointed.

5. Excluding the recesses from 2005 to the present becomes necessary because the number of executive orders produced in President Bush's second term is not known. As of November, 2007, no additional judicial recess appointments have been made after 2004.

6. Using the Senate recess as the unit of analysis is preferable for a number of reasons. Alternatives, such as aggregating to the year, congressional session, or presidential term would mean discarding valuable variation, especially since we have expectations about the likelihood of a recess appointment given the length of the individual recess, its temporal position in the session, etc. However, collapsing the data to the congressional session, including intersession recesses with the previous session, since the commissions share the same expiration date, the results for the remaining session-level variables are substantially unchanged.

7. This model deals with overdispersion, the greater than expected variation evident in the data, by modifying the conditional mean and variance functions and specifies a separate data generating process for some of the observed zero counts.

8. Coefficients in the zero-inflation equation have a somewhat counter-intuitive interpretation. The coefficients represent the estimates of a logit equation on the production of zero-count recesses, so a positive coefficient reflects an increase in the likelihood of observing a recess in the "zero-state." Likewise, a negative coefficient indicates that the

variable in question is inversely related to the observation of recesses in the zero-state. Other alternative specifications, such as including interactions of all the variables in the outcome and inflation equations with the modern presidency and including the exposure covariate in the inflation equation, produced substantively similar results although the former approach produced signs of convergence problems. Also, we re-estimated the model excluding the Truman and Kennedy outlier recesses featuring 23 and 22 recess appointments respectively as a sensitivity check. The results produced only one substantive difference: the intra-session recesses variable in the count outcome equation was no longer statistically significant at an alpha=.05 level (one-tailed).

9. Length of Senate recess enters the equation logged (ln[days Senate is in recess]) to account for the likelihood of a nonlinear effect. Using the raw number of days the Senate is in recess produces very similar results, but an inferior model in terms of log likelihood and information criteria.

10. The length of recesses enters the model logged, so an increase of one unit from the average Senate recess length represents a change from about 25 days to about 67 days and a unit decrease is down to 9 days.

Chapter Three

Supreme Court Recess Appointments and Voting

Introduction

It is often taken as axiomatic that an independent judiciary is crucial to a balanced government of separated powers. A truly independent judiciary is free from the "passions" of short-term majorities and can act to protect the interests of electoral and ethnic minorities. In effect, an independent judiciary, although potentially anti-majoritarian, stands ready to protect and defend bedrock democratic principles such as free speech and equal participation in government. The justices of the United States Supreme Court, sitting at the peak of the federal judicial hierarchy, must be responsible for vindicating these principles, even against threats from the government.

Article III of the Constitution creates a judiciary that appears equal to these responsibilities. By its provisions, the judiciary enjoys significant independence compared with historical precursors or with parallel contemporary institutions. Article III prescribes that the justices of the Supreme Court and those holding all other inferior judicial positions created by Congress "shall hold their Offices during good Behavior, and shall, at stated Times, receive for their Services a Compensation which shall not be diminished during their Continuance in Office" (United States Constitution, Article III, Section 1). That is, the Supreme Court and all other Article III federal courts have lifetime tenure and face no realistic threat of retaliation for unpopular rulings or opinions from Congress, the president or the public.

While there has been research and debate as to the extent of judicial independence enjoyed by Article III courts (Rosenberg 1992; but see Segal and Spaeth 2002, chapter 10), there is little debate that the federal courts in the United States enjoy a high degree of independence, especially compared to courts of many other countries (Howard and Carey 2002). However, there is one possible exception to this state of judicial independence—the judge sitting as a recess appointee.

Article II gives the executive the power to "fill up all Vacancies that may happen during the Recess of the Senate, by granting Commissions which shall expire at the End of their next Session." Included in these appointees is the federal judiciary. Thus, the president can use the recess power to bypass the requirement that the Senate confirm appointees. The original purpose of the Recess Appointment Clause is uncontroversial—it allows the executive to keep the operations of government running even when the Senate is not in session. However, presidents now make recess appointments even during relatively brief intrasession breaks of the Senate.

In this chapter, we examine the situation of Supreme Court justices. We explore this issue by examining judicial recess appointees who have later been confirmed by the Senate to full time Article III judicial positions. Specifically we compare the behavior of three recess-appointed Supreme Court justices during their temporary appointment tenure with a similar period following Senate confirmation.

Separation of Powers and Judicial Choice

Judicial independence is just one facet of a larger issue concerning the role of the judiciary within the constitutional system of separated powers. Each branch has overlapping responsibilities and power subject to control and review by the other branches of government. Although this was undoubtedly a deliberate design by the framers to prevent the aggregation of power by any single branch of government, the separation of powers system leads to battles between the courts, Congress, and the executive. The indispensible actor in the exercise of the courts' responsibilities as a coordinate branch under the Constitution is the United States Supreme Court.

Substantial literature has grown around inter-branch politics, producing studies of the branches as political institutions and analyzing how these institutions constrain, define, and mold political behavior. Scholars working within a rational choice framework often view these interactions as a game with a series of sequential moves by each branch of government and have shown that the policy choice of a governmental actor or institution results from not just from the policy preference of the actor but also a calculation as to the reactions of other actors and institutions (Vanberg 2000; Epstein and Knight 1998; Ferejohn and Shipan 1990; Eskridge 1991; Rogers 2001; Segal 1997).

Walter Murphy's *Elements of Judicial Strategy* (1964) is widely recognized as an important early examination of strategic Supreme Court decision making. Murphy details the strategy of the opinion writing process, and judicial anticipation of how other political actors would respond to their decisions. In addition to anecdotal evidence, Murphy utilized Court memos and draft opinions in order to explore the various ways justices attempted to actualize their policy preferences given the complicated and intricate web of constraints presented by the American system.

Building on this and other works, Epstein and Knight (1998) contend that strategic considerations lie at the core of judicial voting. One part of their analysis focused on two pairs of famous cases with similar facts yet opposite outcomes. The first pair they examined was the Civil War habeas cases of *Ex Parte Milligan* (1866) and *Ex Parte McCardle* (1869). The second pair was the cold war congressional subpoena cases of *Watkins v. United States* (1957) and *Barenblatt v. United States* (1959). In both pairs of cases the Court supported the right of the individual in the first case, but was challenged by Congress and backed the government's position in the second. Following *Milligan*, Congress stripped the courts of jurisdiction to hear these types of cases, while after *Watkins*, Congress threatened similar jurisdiction stripping legislation. Epstein and Knight argue that the justices changed from their sincere preference of supporting individual rights to backing the government because of the pressure from Congress that threatened the independence of the Court. These examples, chosen for their expository clarity, also highlight the normative issues raised by circumstances that threaten the independence of the judiciary.

An Overview of Judicial Recess Appointments

With the exception of John Tyler and William Henry Harrison (who died in office after only 30 days) all presidents in the eighteenth and nineteenth centuries used the recess appointment power. For example, George Washington made nine recess appointments, including the appointment of three judges to the Federal District Court during the recess of the First Congress. Presidents have made over three hundred recess appointments to the federal judiciary and fifteen Supreme Court justices have initially been seated through the recess appointment power. We list these justices in Table 3.1.

As we can see, the Recess Appointment Clause has been invoked to appoint justices with some regularity, particularly in the early days of the Republic. George Washington exercised its authority three times to appoint justices to the Supreme Court, although confirmation failed in the case of John Rutledge. John Adams, Thomas Jefferson, and John Quincy Adams all appointed Supreme Court justices while the Senate was out of session. Several justices usually ranked as great or near great received their initial appointments through the recess power. Included among these are Justices Oliver Wendell Holmes, the first Justice John Harlan, Earl Warren, and William Brennan (Pederson and Provizer 2003).

After the recess appointment of Oliver Wendell Holmes by Theodore Roosevelt—an appointment Roosevelt would come to regret[1] (Abraham 1999)—the practice of appointing Supreme Court justices temporarily without Senate action entered a moratorium lasting for 51 years (Stanford Law Review 1957). However, President Dwight D. Eisenhower broke with this unwritten protocol and ap-

Table 3.1: Supreme Court Recess Appointments		
Supreme Court Justice	Date of Recess Appointment	Result
Stewart, Potter	10/14/1958	Confirmed 5/5/1959
Brennan, William J.	10/15/1956	Confirmed 3/19/1957
Warren, Earl	10/2/1953	Confirmed 3/1/1954
Holmes, Oliver W.	8/11/1902	Confirmed 12/4/1902
Harlan, John M.	3/29/1877	Confirmed 11/29/1877
Davis, David	10/17/1862	Confirmed 12/8/1862
Curtis, Benjamin R.	9/22/1851	Confirmed 12/20/1851
Woodbury, Levi	9/20/1845	Confirmed 1/3/1846
McKinley, John	4/22/1837	Confirmed 9/25/1837
Thompson, Smith	9/1/1823	Confirmed 12/19/1823
Livingston, Henry B.	11/10/1806	Confirmed 12/17/1806
Moore, Alfred	10/20/1799	Confirmed 12/10/1799
Washington, Bushrod	9/29/1798	Confirmed 12/20/1798
Rutledge, John	7/1/1795	Failed, expired 12/15/1795
Johnson, Thomas	8/5/1791	Confirmed 11/7/1791

pointed three justices to the United States Supreme Court, to wit, Chief Justice Earl Warren and Associate Justices William Brennan and Potter Stewart.

Judicial recess appointments are not innovative or untraditional uses of the president's constitutional authority, but they are controversial and, within the context of modern congressional-executive relations, problematic. Controversies over judicial recess appointments are not an entirely new phenomenon. One of President Washington's recess appointments was of John Rutledge to chief justice of the United States, igniting a controversy, which, according to Curtis (1984), contributed to his rejection by the Senate.

Uses of the recess appointment power in recent decades have triggered substantial debate about the propriety and wisdom of the exercise of the recess appointment power. Following President Eisenhower's third placement of a Supreme Court justice during a recess, the Senate passed a resolution opposing the practice.[2] The resolution stated that recess appointments to the Supreme Court should be used only "under unusual and urgent circumstances" and the corresponding report from the Judiciary Committee asserted that such appointments obstructed the Senate's "solemn constitutional task" of providing advice and consent.[3] Despite the institutional prerogatives asserted, however, the resolution passed on a primarily partisan vote, 48 to 37 (Fisher 2005).

While the United States Senate's primary concern with the recess appointment of Supreme Court justices might be protecting institutional prerogatives and power, a recess appointment suggests other normative concerns about judicial voting and behavior. Specifically, there is the potential for an adverse impact on judicial independence. Judicial independence is an essential component of our legal system. Its goal is impartial, "law-based" decision making by judges, decisions made without regard for the political preferences of members of the other branches. "The judiciary," Gerald Rosenberg writes, "is independent to the extent its decision-making is free from domination by the preferences of elected officials" (Rosenberg 1992, 371). Others define judicial independence as "a condition in which judges are entirely free from negative consequences for their decisions on the bench," (Baum 2003) or "the ability of the individual judge to make decisions based on the facts and the law without undue influence or interference" (Zemans 1999).

Increasingly, unpopular decisions have led to calls for greater political control over the judiciary, leading to a debate over the proper balance between judicial independence and judicial accountability. Recently United States District Court Judge Harold Baer generated both a suggestion from the president that he consider resigning and a presidential candidate's call for his impeachment when he granted a suppression motion (Van Natta, Jr. 1996). In response, Chief Judge John O. Newman of the Second Circuit Court of Appeals and three former chief judges issued a joint statement, asserting that "when a judge is threatened with a call for resignation or impeachment because of disagreement with a ruling, the entire process of orderly resolution of legal disputes is undermined" (Van Natta, Jr. quoting Newman 1996).

In part, judicial independence is a function of institutional structures. The Constitution creates a federal judiciary as a separate and co-equal branch, a branch given the power of judicial review. Article III of the United States Constitution preserves the independence of judges in their decision making process by guaranteeing a lifetime appointment and salaries that may not be diminished. In theory, this independence, plus the power of judicial review, allows the judiciary to "stand as the ultimate guardians of our fundamental rights" (Horsky 1958, 1111). Thus, judicial independence allows judges to uphold minority rights when they are under attack. However, Ferejohn (1999) suggests that the independence of the judiciary is threatened if Congress and the president are ideologically unified and the judiciary is comprised of judges with a different ideology. In addition, Rosenberg (1999) examines nine periods of intense Court-curbing activity along with the Supreme Court decisions during those periods. He finds that in only three of the nine periods was the Supreme Court clearly independent of congressional preferences, rejecting the notion that independence is a status quo.

Chapter 3

In fact, judicial independence lay at the heart of two court cases challenging recess appointments, one by President Jimmy Carter and the most recent recess appointment of William Pryor by George W. Bush. On January 1, 1981, President Jimmy Carter recess appointed Walter Heen to the U.S. District Court for the District of Hawaii. Judge Heen then presided over the trial and conviction of Janet Woodley on drug charges. In *United States v. Woodley* (1982) the Ninth Circuit analyzed the inherent tension between the President's recess appointment power under Article II which gives the Executive the power to "fill up all Vacancies that may happen during the Recess of the Senate, by granting Commissions which shall expire at the End of their next Session" and the attributes of judicial independence incorporated into Article III. It held that "only those judges enjoying Article III protections may exercise the judicial power of the United States" and vacated the lower court decision. According to the court, "[a] judge receiving his commission under the Recess Appointment Clause may be called upon to make politically charged decisions while his nomination awaits approval by popularly elected officials. Such a judge will scarcely be oblivious to the effect his decision may have on the vote of these officials." (726 F. 2nd 1328, 1330) When a recess appointee hears a case, he or she does not have a permanent appointment and whether the appointee receives tenure is still contingent upon renomination by the president and confirmation by the Senate (Mayton 2004).

As we noted in our introduction, the Ninth Circuit then reheard the case *en banc* and reversed. This was not the first time the idea was broached that unconfirmed judges might be subject to unacceptable political pressures. At Justice Stewart's confirmation hearing, the dissent to his confirmation argued that the right to a trial before a life-appointed judge is just as much a constitutional right as the right of trial by jury in criminal cases (Mayton 2004). In fact, after the Stewart confirmation hearings, the Senate Judiciary Committee submitted a resolution to the Senate, discouraging recess appointments to the Supreme Court.[4] Specifically, there was concern about the propriety of a judge hearing cases prior to confirmation.

> A litigant "may for the rest of his life wonder" whether his case was influenced, consciously, or unconsciously, by the temporary judge's knowledge that he must please the President, so that he does withdraw the judge's nomination, and the Senate, so that it confirms him. The judge might bend to these pressures or he might do the opposite; he "might rear back and bend the other way to prove that we was subservient to neither branch (Mayton 2004, 538).

Of course these concerns lead to a simple, yet important question. Do judicial recess appointees behave differently during the recess appointment than they do as fully independent judges? Are the complaints of litigants and the fears of court observers that diminishing the constitutional protections of judges' independence compromises the exercise of judicial power justified?

There is evidence that judicial independence is comparatively diminished without the protections given by the United States Constitution. For example, Salzberger and Fenn (1999) show that judges on the English Court of Appeals who consistently take antigovernment positions are less likely to be promoted to the Judicial Committee of the House of Lords, the highest judicial venue in England, than lord justices of appeal who are less antigovernment. Similarly, Ramseyer (1994) and Ramseyer and Rasmusen (1997) show that antigovernment judges in Japan experience less successful and more unpleasant careers than do pro-government judges.

In the United States the other branches have control over jurisdiction, appointment, enforcement of court rulings, appropriations for the operation of the courts, and can impeach judges. Thus, there are many ways in which Congress and the president can exert influence over the federal judiciary. For example, legislation restricting judicial review of habeas corpus petitions, sentencing guidelines that include mandatory minimums that severely limit judicial discretion and the Civil Justice Reform Act of 1990 that imposed oversight by district level committees and mandated alternative resolution programs has been adopted (Zemans 1999).

At the state level, the opportunities for influence are even greater given the different election systems. In a series of articles, Hall (1987, 1992) and Brace and Hall (1995, 1997) have shown state high court vote choice can depend on party competition, electoral consequences, and citizen ideology. In short, judges who must run in retention elections and for reelection exhibit different voting patterns than appointed judges who thus have greater independence from the consequences of their decisions.

Thus, the process by which judges are appointed and retained can have an impact on judicial independence and accountability. When presidents and Senators subject judicial nominees to ideological "litmus tests," they are routinely accused of undermining the nominees' independence, while the presidents and Senators assert that asking about a nominee's "judicial philosophy" is a way to gauge whether the nominees are acceptable (Geyh 2003).

Similar patterns exist for recess appointees. Jefferson B. Fordham, dean of the University of Pennsylvania Law School, remarked that a recess appointee "is serving under the overhang of Senate consideration of a nomination, which is not in harmony with the constitutional policy of judiciary independence."[5] Herz (2005, 450) argues that "circumstances put the recess appointee in something of the same position as a law professor on a 'look-see visit'; his or her job becomes one extended interview. These circumstances are utterly at odds with the commitment to judicial independence reflected in Article III's good behavior clause and salary protections."

While recess appointed justices will not have to confront the electorate, existing research on court nominations, judicial behavior, and judicial voting provides insight that buttresses the assertion noted above. Assuming that a recess appointee wants confirmation, the "electorate" that the nominee would care about most is the Senate. Research has shown that the median ideology of the Senate (Moraski and Shipan 1999) or even the partisan make-up of the Senate (Epstein and Segal 2005) can be critical to confirmation of the nominee as the president and Senate clash over the nominee, each seeking an ideological advantage in the separation of powers struggles (Yates and Whitford 1998). The more liberal or Democratic the Senate the greater is the likelihood that the recess appointee would vote in a more liberal direction. One might also see a liberal or conservative recess appointee retreat to the ideological center.

Ideological voting is not the only way a recess-appointed justice could assuage Senate concerns. He would also likely avoid controversial rulings or behavior that would lead to unwanted attention. This could include avoiding separate opinion writing or controversial votes, such as overturning precedent or state or federal law, or ruling against the state or federal government. We also anticipate that the recess appointee would also be more likely to vote with the majority during the period of their recess appointment.

Research on other courts confirms some of these suspicions. For example, research on appellate court behavior shows that district court judges sitting by designation on the appellate court are less likely to issue separate opinions or otherwise engage in more dissensus oriented behavior (Hettinger et al. 2006). In addition, a recess appointee might not want to alienate a senator by joining a decision to limit state or federal authority.

Recess-Appointed Supreme Court Justices: A Brief Review

In the post-War era, three Supreme Court justices have received recess appointments, Chief Justice Earl Warren, Justice William Brennan, and Justice Potter Stewart, each appointed in October of 1953, 1956, and 1958, respectively. Each sat on the bench for five to seven months before receiving confirmation by the Senate. Before Chief Justice Warren, the most recent recess appointment to the Supreme Court was of Oliver Wendell Holmes in 1902, well before the earliest point at which case-vote level data for the Supreme Court are readily available. In order to isolate the possible effects of sitting via temporary appointment, we wish to compare the behavior of these justices under this condition with an appropriate benchmark, similar behavior without the condition.

The Appointment of Earl Warren

Warren was a dominant political figure in California politics with his political positions moving from traditional Republican views to a prominent position as a leader of the progressive wing of the Republican Party (Schwartz 1996). He obtained his law degree from the University of California Berkeley's newly opened law school in 1914 and after service in the army quickly moved up the political ladder in California politics, from district attorney to attorney general to governor of the state, in the process was nominated by both the Democratic and Republican party in 1946 and easily beating Franklin D. Roosevelt's son James in the 1950 gubernatorial election.

An aspirant for the presidential nomination in both 1948 and 1952, Warren reportedly threw his support to Eisenhower over that of Senator Robert A. Taft of Ohio and for that was promised the first vacancy to occur on the United States Supreme Court (Schwartz 1996, 438), although Abraham dismisses this story and argues that Warren's appointment to the Court was as much to remove him from California politics than any deal to secure the presidency for Eisenhower (Abraham 1999, 192-193).

With the sudden death of Chief Justice Vinson in September of 1953 a vacancy opened up on the Supreme Court and Eisenhower used the recess power to quickly fill the position less than one month later with Earl Warren. Although eventually confirmed to the position by a unanimous voice vote in March, 1954, Warren's recess nomination led to some initial opposition by Senator William Langer of North Dakota, who apparently, was opposed to the nomination of anyone not from North Dakota (Abraham 1999, 194) and some Southern Democrats concerned over Warren's liberal views. Thus Warren was on the bench for several months while awaiting confirmation.

The Appointment of William Brennan

Brennan's appointment, like that of Earl Warren, also had the appearance of political considerations. Brennan, the son of working class Irish immigrants grew up in a large Catholic family in Newark, New Jersey. His father became active in local Democratic politics and eventually ran and won office to the Newark Board of Commissioners with Brennan helping out in the campaign.

Despite his father's desire to see his son in a business career, William Brennan opted to enroll in Harvard Law School after graduating from the University of Pennsylvania. Following graduation and after a stint in the Army during World War II, Brennan practiced law before being named to the Superior Court of New Jersey by Republican Governor Alfred Driscoll in 1949, following successful efforts to help reform the New Jersey court system and establishing a pattern of Republican political support for his judicial aspirations. For example, soon thereafter, Brennan became an ally, trusted lieutenant, and eventually right-hand man to the Republican chief justice of the New Jersey Supreme Court, Arthur Vanderbilt. By 1952 with Vanderbilt's backing, Brennan was appointed to the New Jersey high court.

Following Sherman Minton's death in April 1956, Eisenhower had an opening for an Associate Justice on the United States Supreme Court. Eisenhower sought to quickly fill the position and had political considerations in mind as he approached reelection for his second term. Brennan, a northeastern Catholic Democrat, offered several politically appealing traits to Eisenhower's reelection efforts and met the state criteria of relative youth, judicial experience, and high state bar standing (Abraham 1999). Vanderbilt strongly supported Brennan's nomination. Thus Eisenhower nominated Brennan during an October Senate recess, shortly before the presidential election in November, and formally nominated him with the congressional session of January 1957, and was confirmed two months later on a voice vote with the only dissent coming from Senator Joseph McCarthy (Wermiel 1996).

The Appointment of Potter Stewart

Stewart was the fifth and last nomination of President Eisenhower. Stewart fits the traditional mold of a politically connected nominee. Born into a well-to-do family prominent in both law and Ohio Republican politics, Stewart enjoyed an affluent childhood and privileged education that included a prestigious prep school, The Hotchkiss School in Lakeville, Connecticut. While the Great Depression brought financial hardship to his family, Stewart was able to secure scholarship aid to finish prep school and enroll at Yale. Following a year of study abroad, Stewart entered Yale Law School, eventually becoming editor of the Yale Law Journal.

Following corporate practice and a stint in the Navy during World War II, Stewart entered into politics and supported Eisenhower's 1952 presidential bid over that of Ohio native son, Robert Taft. Upon the recommendation of Ohio Republican Senator John W. Bricker, Stewart was appointed by President Eisenhower to the Sixth Circuit Court of Appeals in 1954. At the time he was the youngest judge on the Court.

When fellow Ohioan Harold H. Burton retired on October 13, 1958, due to ill health, Eisenhower immediately filled the vacancy with the recess appointment of Potter Stewart. Although Stewart's qualifications were never an issue, the nomination did run into some trouble with Southern Democrats concerned over Stewart's obvious commitment to civil rights and desegregation. Several southern senators then were able to delay the confirmation vote for several months. The judiciary committee eventually reported favorably on the nomination by a twelve to three vote, with three Southern Democratic senators dissenting. The full Senate confirmed Stewart by a vote of seventy to seventeen in May of 1959.

Hypotheses

We specify several hypotheses about several political and institutional factors that we expect to have an impact on the behavior of these justices before confirmation and afterward. Our first set of hypotheses relate to how likely the justices are to cast liberal votes in given circumstances.

Hypothesis 1: A recess appointee will be less likely to cast liberal votes before Senate confirmation.

Hypothesis 2: A recess appointee will be more likely to cast liberal votes when the Senate is controlled by the Democratic Party before Senate confirmation.

Hypothesis 3: A recess appointee will be less likely to cast liberal votes in cases that are publicly salient before Senate confirmation.

Hypothesis 4: A recess appointee will be more likely to cast liberal votes as the number of other justices in a liberal majority coalition increases before Senate confirmation.

We stipulate a second set of hypotheses concerning the propensity of the justices to cast votes to affirm based on several conditions of the cases and the institutional context, pre- and post-confirmation.

Hypothesis 5: A recess appointee will be less likely to cast votes to affirm when the United States appears as the petitioner/appellant before Senate confirmation.

Hypothesis 6: A recess appointee will be less likely to cast votes to affirm when a state appears as the petitioner/appellant before Senate confirmation.

Hypothesis 7: A recess appointee will be less likely to cast votes to affirm when the United States appears as the respondent/appellant before Senate confirmation.

Hypothesis 8: A recess appointee will be less likely to cast votes to affirm when a state appears as the respondent/appellant before Senate confirmation.

43

Hypothesis 9: A recess appointee will be more likely to cast votes to affirm when the decision the Court is reviewing affirmed the judgment of the Court below before Senate confirmation.

Hypothesis 10: A recess appointee will be more likely to cast votes to affirm as the number of other justices in an affirm majority coalition increases before Senate confirmation.

Data and Analysis

President Dwight Eisenhower appointed each of these justices, so there is no variation in appointing president among our subjects. However, all three of Eisenhower's high court recess appointments went on to successful confirmation after spending five to seven months as an active participant in cases. Each justice's continued tenure in the Court depended on the nomination and support of the president and the consent of the Senate during these months. Because each of these justices spent a considerable portion of their first terms as recess appointees, we can compare their behavior during their recess periods with their behavior post-confirmation.

Using the Spaeth Supreme Court Database, converted to justice as the unit of analysis by Sarah Benesh and Chris Zorn, we gathered data on each of the justices from the date they arrived on the bench to the date they were confirmed by the Senate. We also collected data from a similar number of case-votes of the same justices in the months immediately following their confirmation. In addition to case factors, the database contains indicators of the directions of the justices' votes in ideological terms—liberal or conservative—and in terms of the disposition for the lower court's decision—affirm or reverse.

We considered and rejected contrasting the justices' pre-confirmation behavior with the remainder of their careers on the bench. While this would make use of as much information as is available about their performance while enjoying life tenure, we cannot be certain that votes made years after the recess period are truly comparable. Changes in the institution of the Court, the dynamics of small-group decision-making, the political context, and the legal agenda facing the justices could all change, confounding recess effects. Furthermore, several studies indicate that many justices demonstrate ideological change over time on the bench, which manifests itself in behavioral changes (Epstein and Knight 1998; Martin and Quinn 2002). Finally, many court scholars find that certain justices are prone to acclimation effects, changes in their behavior as they adjust to their new role and setting, although such periods of adjustment are thought to take a full term or two before noticeable differences appear (Hagle 1993; Hurwitz and Stefko 2004). This issue in particular cautions against casting too far from the recess period for comparable observations. Votes were considered "before" or "after" confirmation depending on the report date for the vote, rather than the conference date, because for several cases exact conference date information was not available and justices are always free to change their votes until the report date (Howard 1968).

For Warren and Brennan, the inclusion of the remainder of their initial terms on the bench produced as many or more post-confirmation votes. Justice Stewart, however, was not confirmed until rather late in his first term of service. In the 1958 term, Stewart cast 75 votes before confirmation and only 46 votes following. To estimate pre- and post-confirmation behavior for Stewart with comparable precision, we included several decision days from the 1959 term, adding 25 votes to nearly equalize the two sets (the latest votes for Stewart were reported January 10th, 1960). The periods and number of votes for each justice are summarized in Table 3.2.

Our data come from three justices appointed by a Republican president, albeit one who by reputation did not make ideology a high priority for judicial appointments (Epstein and Segal 2005). Two of those appointments faced a very closely divided Senate, only one controlled by the president's party, while the third justice's nomination (Stewart) was considered by a newly elected and substantial Democratic majority. To gain a better understanding of the extent to which being a recess appointee affects the behavior of the justices, we analyze the impact of political and case factors on their voting before and after their confirmation.

Influences Before and After Confirmation

Justices on the Supreme Court are expected to be relatively free of external influences, free to carry out the judicial function, address fundamental questions of law and policy, and confront the political branches when necessary despite controversy. We suspect, however, that when justices are recess appointees, they will be less inclined to take actions or positions that expose them to public attention or criticism from within the executive or legislative branches. To what fac-

Table 3.2: Eisenhower Supreme Court Justices Seated via Recess Appointment				
Justice	Recess Appt. Date	Confirmation Date	Votes during Recess Appt.	Votes following Recess Appt.[1]
Earl Warren	10/2/1953	3/1/1954	39	41
William Brennan	10/15/1956	3/19/1957	46	69
Potter Stewart	10/14/1958	5/5/1959	75 (74)[2]	71 (70)[2]

[1]For Warren and Brennan, votes following recess appointment are all remaining votes for the justices' first term. For Stewart, additional opinion days from his second term were included until the number of "after confirmation" votes nearly equaled the number of "before confirmation" votes.
[2]Two votes for Stewart, one before confirmation and one after, have no liberal-conservative coding.

Chapter 3

tors, we ask, do justices respond when sitting temporarily that they would feel free to disregard with the security of life tenure? In order to address this question, we specified several maximum likelihood models of justices' votes, comparing the influences of various factors before and after the justices are confirmed.

Descriptive statistics for the variables used in our models appear in Tables 3.3 and 3.4. We analyze the justices' tendencies toward liberal voting and their choices to affirm or reverse. Other variables we use include the size of the liberal voting majority in the case, if the case is decided liberally, whether the federal government or a state appear in the case as petitioners or respondents, and the ideological direction of the lower court, as well as an indicator of whether or not the Democrats controlled the Senate at the time. Table 3.3 breaks down a set of case and contextual factor indicators across the confirmation line. Because most of the pre-confirmation votes come from relatively early in the terms and most of the post-confirmation votes come from their last months, we observe some differences. Publicly salient cases, measured by coverage in the *New York Times*, are more common late in the term and are thus more frequent after confirmation. We cannot discount the possibility that announcement of some of these cases were delayed until after recessed justices were confirmed. Most of the other variables are distributed similarly across samples, differing only by small fractions of their sizes.

The next table, 3.4, presents the same variables across justices, or terms. Again, while we find some differences across terms, none that generate reliability or validity concerns. Media coverage appears to be constant, but the size of the successful liberal voting blocs increase from Warren's initial term to Bren-

Table 3.3: Descriptive Statistics – Pooled, Before, and After Confirmation						
Factor	Pooled		Before Confirmation		After Confirmation	
	Mean	Std. Dev.	Mean	Std. Dev.	Mean	Std. Dev.
Liberal Votes	.566	.496	.577	.495	.556	.498
Democratic Senate	.746	.425	.745	.437	.781	.415
Public Salience (*NYT*)	.145	.352	.093	.292	.191	.394
Liberal Majority Size	.445	.327	.465	.397	.428	.383
Affirm Votes	.119	.214	.420	.495	.402	.492
U.S. Petitioner	.737	.441	.186	.391	.225	.419
State Petitioner	.068	.252	.043	.205	.045	.208
U.S. Respondent	.052	.223	.342	.476	.292	.456
State Respondent	.359	.480	.441	.498	.449	.499
Lower Court Direction (Affirm)	.348	.477	.379	.487	.320	.468
Affirm Majority Size	.302	.364	.333	.378	.274	3.350
	N = 996		N = 375		N = 621	

Table 3.4: Descriptive Statistics – by Justice/Term						
Factor	Warren (1953)		Brennan (1956)		Stewart (1958/9)	
	Mean	Std. Dev.	Mean	Std. Dev.	Mean	Std. Dev.
Public Salience (*NYT*)	.138	.347	.157	.365	.139	.347
Liberal Majority Size	.353	.397	.492	.372	.459	.394
U.S. Petitioner	.238	.428	.217	.414	.178	.384
State Petitioner	.038	.191	.026	.160	.075	.265
U.S. Respondent	.250	.436	.348	.478	.321	.469
State Respondent	.400	.493	.443	.499	.473	.501

nan and Stewart's. We detect some differences in the appearances of government litigants from term to term, as the United States is seen more often as respondent and less as petitioner in 1956 than three terms earlier. The trend for states is consistently upward. States are more frequently petitioners and respondents in cases late in the decade. None of the differences are extraordinary, however.

Our first analysis is of liberal-conservative voting, as coded in the Spaeth Database. The dependent variable, coded one for a liberal vote and zero for a conservative vote, is dichotomous, thus we use a logit model. We fashioned hypotheses about the expected direction of various influences on Supreme Court justices before and after confirmation, but what we are really interested in is whether the influences of various factors on justices' votes are different from each other before and after confirmation. Thus, our approach is to specify a model of justices' votes that captures the potential impact of external influences or undesirable attention and test whether the coefficients estimated from that specification differs across groups of votes: those made during the recess appointment period and those made after Senate confirmation.

A standard approach to testing whether the same coefficients govern the relationships between a set of covariates and the outcome across two different groups of observations is to conduct a Chow test (Chow 1960). The F-distributed Chow test is often referred to as a test of the "pooling assumption" or a test of "structural change," and is equivalent to an F-test of a fully interactive model pooling both sets of data. Unfortunately, as Allison (1999) notes, in discrete choice models such as logit, the validity of hypothesis tests using variables interacted across different groups of data relies on the assumption that the residual variation in data is equivalent between groups. Further studies have revealed that if this assumption is violated, naïve hypothesis tests of such interactive effects and the Chow test can give misleading results, perhaps even contrary to the actual relationships in the data (Hoetker 2007).

Heterogeneous choice models allow the variance of discrete choice models to vary as a function of a set of specified covariates, which can be indicators of group membership or other characteristics of the observations (Williams 2006).

In political science, the heteroskedastic probit model (Alvarez and Brehm 1995) is probably the most widely familiar variant of this family of models. Specifying a variance function can make outcome coefficients robust in the face of non-constant residual variation, as is the case here, or because variance is itself of substantive interest (as was the case in Alvarez and Brehm's application.) In the models we present, we find significantly non-constant residual variation across confirmation status and present results from heterogeneous logit models that take account of those differences. We do not report the coefficients for the variance function as it is not the focus of our interest.

We wish to capture the conditional effects of these variables—their influences on vote choices before confirmation and following confirmation. Thus, we specify conditional models, estimating separate coefficients for the variables in each condition. We employ two complementary strategies: a "multiplicative interaction" model and a "regime" model. The former is the traditional "interactive" model widely used in social sciences. Variables whose effects are thought to depend on the value of another variable are multiplied by that variable and the resulting term added to the specification. The un-multiplied terms are referred to as the "constituent" terms while the new terms are the "interactions." The second approach is useful when the condition upon which other effects are thought to depend is discrete, as it is here. We produce the "regime" model by multiplying the constituent terms by two variables indicating whether a vote was made before or after confirmation and enter those two sets of covariates into the model in place of the constituent terms. Thus, in the regime model, one set of covariates take their observed values for the before confirmation votes and are zero otherwise, while the other set take their observed values only after confirmation. The regime model allows us to estimate separate marginal effects on the outcome for the covariates across conditions (before and after confirmation) without the complications of the traditional interaction model (Brambor, Clark, and Golder 2006, 69).

As a basis for comparison, we estimated a logit model pooling the pre- and post-confirmation votes, allowing only the constant to vary across these conditions. The standard errors for this and the two subsequent models are heteroskedasticity-robust, clustered on the individual justices. The results appear in the first column of Table 3.5.

Both intercepts are significant and negative, suggesting that the justices did not tend to cast liberal votes, conditional on the other factors. Senate control by the Democrats and public salience are both not statistically significant, but the proportion of the Court joining a liberal majority is significant and appears substantively large. Perhaps unsurprisingly, these justices were more likely to cast liberal votes when their colleagues did so.

The first conditional model is reported in the second column of results. The pre-confirmation intercept remains significant and negative, although the intercept for post-confirmation votes is not significant and much smaller. With other

Table 3.5: Heterogeneous Logit Models of Liberal Vote

Variables	Pooled Model Coefficient (Z)	Interaction Model Coefficient (Z)	Regime Model Coefficient (Z)	$\beta_{Pre} \neq \beta_{Post}$ χ^2
Pre-Confirmation Intercept	-1.460*** (-6.13)	-1.745*** (-9.32)	-1.745*** (-9.32)	
Democratic Senate	-0.690 (-1.00)	-0.0914 (-0.16)	-0.0914 (-0.16)	
Salience (*New York Times* Measure)	-0.553 (-1.18)	-2.0173*** (-10.35)	-2.0173*** (-10.35)	
Liberal Majority Size	5.442*** (6.87)	5.433*** (9.77)	5.433*** (9.77)	
Post-Confirmation Intercept	-1.295*** (-5.62)	-0.049 (-0.22)	-0.049 (-0.22)	7.95***
Democratic Senate Post-Confirmation		0.012 (0.02)	-0.0602*** (-8.11)	0.00
Salience (*NYT*) Post-Confirmation		2.028*** (7.69)	0.00859 (0.23)	75.99***
Liberal Majority Size Post-Confirmation		-5.085*** (-8.11)	0.264** (2.45)	61.90***
Log-Likelihood (Null = -231.981)	-129.134	-125.815	-125.815	

* p < .10; ** p < .05, *** p < .01, Two-tailed tests; SEs clustered on justice and heteroskedasticity-robust. Coefficients are adjusted for non-constant residual variation across confirmation status. Variance equation omitted.

factors accounted for across conditions, it seems that the justices were not generally inclined against liberal votes after they were confirmed. The liberal majority size coefficient is virtually unchanged from the pooled model, but public salience, operationalized by appearance of the case on the front page of the *New York Times*, is significant and negative. Before confirmation, recess-appointed justices are less likely to cast liberal votes when the Court's decision is highly newsworthy.

In this model, the interactive terms represent the departures from the estimated constituent effects for votes cast after confirmation rather than marginal effects. Interpreting the estimated effects of changes in the variables on liberal voting requires taking account of both estimated effects, and assessment of whether those effects are statistically significant requires calculation of compound standard errors taking account of the covariance of the estimated effects. If anything, the coefficients and test statistics of interaction terms might reveal whether the marginal effects of the constituent terms are significantly conditional on each other, although perhaps not even that (Brambor et al. 2006, 74).

The third column of results contains the coefficients of the "regime" specification. In this model, the estimated effects of the post-confirmation variables are marginal effects, rather than interactive departures from the constituent effects. There are observable differences between each of the coefficients and these differences are very revealing. The intercepts are noticeably distinct, significantly so, and the pre-confirmation baseline is substantially more negative, indicating that the justices were considerably more likely to cast liberal votes after they were confirmed. The variable indicating a Senate controlled by the Democrats is not significant in the pre-confirmation specification, but the post-confirmation effect is significant and negative, although its substantive impact is not great. Consistent with the interaction results, the coefficients for public salience are profoundly dissimilar. Pre-confirmation, in cases salience to the public, measured by being reported on the front page of the *New York Times*, are significantly less likely to prompt a liberal vote. Post-confirmation, however, this effect is insignificant and vanishingly small.

To demonstrate the impact of public salience on liberal voting before and after the justices receive permanent tenure, Figure 3.1 shows the changes in the predicted probability of a liberal vote for non-salient and salient cases across confirmation status.

All other variables in the model are fixed at their central values, median or mean. The leftmost bar shows the likelihood of a liberal vote before confirmation for a "typical" non-salient case, which is above .6, or 60 percent. A salient case, pre-confirmation, has a substantially lower probability of eliciting a liberal vote, less than .2. The two bars corresponding to vote probabilities post-confirmation, for salient and non-salient cases, are practically identical, however-er.

The size of the voting majority in liberally decided cases is also statistically significant pre-confirmation, but insignificant following confirmation. To demonstrate this effect visually, Figure 3.2 graphs the predicted likelihood of a liberal vote across a range of values for the size of the majority in a case decided

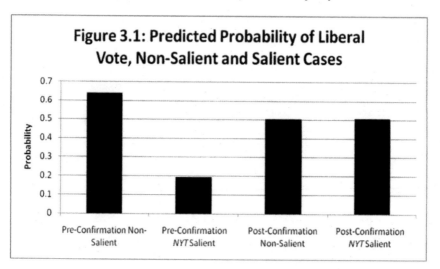

Figure 3.1: Predicted Probability of Liberal Vote, Non-Salient and Salient Cases

liberally. Before confirmation, the predicted probability increases from about 65 percent when the number of liberal votes cast by the other justices is equal to 4 (some cases in our dataset are decided by a less-than-full Court, meaning that a case receiving only four liberal votes could be decided liberally even without the vote of the recess-appointed justice). As the size of the liberal majority increases, however, the likelihood of the recess-appointed justice casting a liberal vote increases as well, approaching 100 percent when all of the justice's fellows vote. In contrast, recess appointed justices after confirmation are virtually unaffected by the number of other justices on the Court casting liberal votes. In addition to our analysis of liberal voting, we also conducted an examination of voting to affirm cases before the Court by the justices receiving recess appointments. The results of this analysis appear in Table 3.6. As before, the estimates are adjusted for non-constant residual variation.

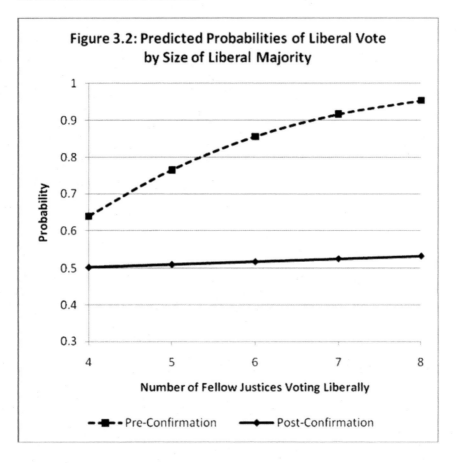

Figure 3.2: Predicted Probabilities of Liberal Vote by Size of Liberal Majority

Table 3.6: Heterogeneous Logit Models of Affirm Vote

Variables	Pooled Model	Interaction Model	Regime Model	
	Coefficient (Z)	Coefficient (Z)	Coefficient (Z)	$\beta_{Pre} \neq \beta_{Post}$ χ^2
Pre-Confirmation Intercept	-2.068*** (-13.52)	-2.144*** (-17.86)	-2.144*** (-17.86)	
U.S. Petitioner	-0.259 (-0.38)	-0.650 (-0.53)	-0.650 (-0.53)	
State Petitioner	-0.153 (-0.30)	-0.436 (-1.10)	-0.436 (-1.10)	
U.S. Respondent	0.086 (1.62)	0.223*** (3.70)	0.223*** (3.70)	
State Respondent	-0.512 (-0.90)	-0.142 (-0.44)	-0.142 (-0.44)	
Direction of Lower Court Decision (Affirm)	-0.028 (-0.03)	-0.204 (-0.29)	-0.204 (-0.29)	
Affirm Majority Size	5.530*** (23.48)	5.498*** (27.11)	5.498*** (27.11)	
Post-Confirmation Intercept	-1.703*** (-3.50)	-0.278*** (-5.50)	-0.176 (-0.22)	14.65***
U.S. Petitioner Post-Confirmation		0.652 (0.54)	0.002 (0.04)	0.29
State Petitioner Post-Confirmation		0.422 (1.19)	-0.015 (-0.28)	1.47
U.S. Respondent Post-Confirmation		-0.230*** (-3.14)	-0.088 (-0.52)	9.43***
State Respondent Post-Confirmation		0.063 (0.26)	-0.088 (-1.14)	0.05
Lower Court Decision Post-Confirmation		0.223 (0.38)	0.0223 (0.16)	0.15
Affirm Majority Size Post-Confirmation		-4.975*** (-20.97)	0.589 (7.34)	519.45***
Log-Likelihood (Null = -229.459)	-130.608	-128.656	-128.656	

* p < .10; ** p < .05, *** p < .01, Two-tailed tests; SEs clustered on justice and heteroskedasticity-robust. Coefficients are adjusted for non-constant residual variation across confirmation status. Variance equation omitted.

Following the same pattern of our previous analysis, the first column of Table 3.6 contains the results of a model pooling all of the votes of our three justices. Only one of the covariates has a statistically significant effect, although the separate intercept for votes cast after confirmation is significant and negative. Justices Warren, Brennan, and Stewart were more likely to vote to reverse after they were confirmed. Also, the number of justices in majority coalitions voting to affirm a case is also significantly related to the justices' choice to cast an affirm vote.

The second column presents the results of a model interacting the affirm vote specification with the indicator of post-confirmation votes. Among the constituent terms, the presence of the U.S. as a respondent is significant and positive. The interpretation of this finding is that cases in which the United States is defending a favorable decision in the lower court, the justices were observably more likely to cast a vote to affirm the lower court's decision. In other words, while the justices were awaiting action on their nominations by the political branches, they were significantly less likely to vote against the United States when appearing before the Court against an appeal. Also, the justices were significantly more likely to vote to affirm when their brethren did so. The multiplicative interactive terms for each of these variables are also significant and negative. Moreover, the size of the coefficients is roughly equal to the size of the constituent terms. The suggestion of these results is that effects present before confirmation largely disappear following Senate approval.

The third column in Table 3.6 follows the same strategy as in Table 3.5, estimating the separate effects of the variables before and after confirmation. As is to be expected, the results for the pre-confirmation votes are the same as for the constituent terms in the second column. The post-confirmation coefficients, however, yield no reliable estimated effects. Thus, while we can infer a relationship between the U.S. respondent and votes to affirm variables and justices' decisions to cast affirm votes while sitting via recess appointment, no such relationships appear to exist subsequently.

The effects of these two variables are presented graphically in Figures 3.3 and 3.4.

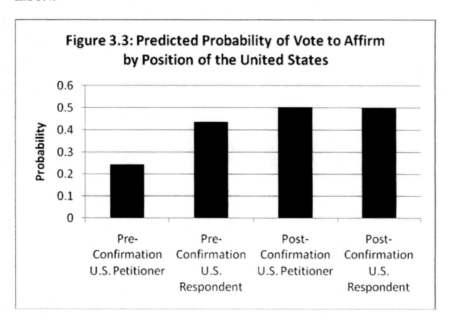

Figure 3.3: Predicted Probability of Vote to Affirm by Position of the United States

The bar graph in Figure 3.3 shows the probabilities of Warren, Brennan, or Stewart voting to affirm a lower court decision before and after confirmation, varying the position of the United States in the case. Figure 3.4 shows the same information in linear format. For cases in which the United States appeared before the Court as a petitioner, seeking to reverse a lower court decision, the justices' predicted probability of voting to affirm was about 25 percent during the recess appointment period, while the estimated likelihood of such a vote when the United States appeared to defend the judgment of the court below is over 40 percent. Following confirmation, the effects of the United States' appearances before the Court were seemingly irrelevant to the justices. Both conditions yield predicted probabilities at almost exactly 50 percent.

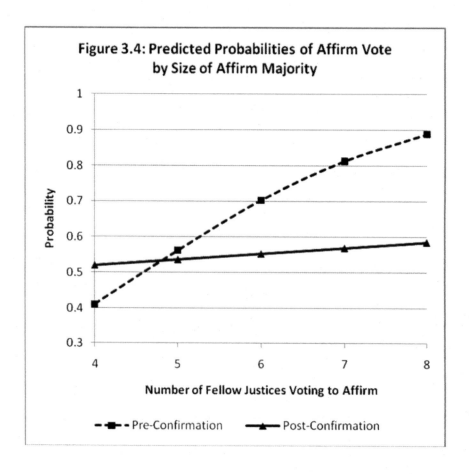

Conclusions

The findings of our analyses indicate that there are differences in the voting records of these Supreme Court justices pre- and post-confirmation. These differences also provide some basis for the sense expressed by the Senate that recess appointments to the Supreme Court are unwise. Our study of ideological voting by the three recess-appointed justices of the Eisenhower administration, Warren, Brennan, and Stewart, reveals that the direction of the justices' votes appeared to be influenced by the salience of the case to the public and the degree of consensus on the Court, but only during their temporary tenures. Following permanent appointment, the estimated effect of these factors disappears.

Given that recess appointees must still receive nomination from the president and be confirmed by the Senate, they lack the independence accorded by the tenure and pay protections of Article III of the United States Constitution. The American system of separated powers is reliant on a vigorous judiciary with the ability and will to check government encroachment on individual liberties and rights, but a recess appointee must be mindful of the Senate, strategically choosing to avoid controversial rulings and behavior that would lead to unwanted attention. Rather than acting sincerely with the protection of life time tenure, the recess appointee must keep "one eye over his shoulder on Congress."

Each of the coordinate branches has overlapping responsibilities and powers subject to control and review by the other branches of government. Although Congress does have some limited checks on the judiciary post-confirmation, and there is evidence that threat of congressional retaliation against the judiciary can constrain the choices of a judge, our analyses indicate that a recess appointee sits in a more precarious position, and, consequently, is less able to fulfill the responsibilities of the judiciary. Specifically, the justices in our study were significantly less likely during their temporary tenure to cast liberal votes in publicly salient cases or when fewer of their colleagues are not voting similarly. Our indicator of public salience, coverage on the front page of the *New York Times*, is likely to identify cases in which the justices would need to cast votes protecting the rights of individuals against government violation, a standard definition of a liberal vote. We also discovered that justices were less likely to vote against the government appearing to defend a favorable lower court judgment during their temporary commissions.

Justices sitting via recess appointment are in a different position than confirmed justices. Our results raise serious concerns about the validity of permitting recess-appointed justices to exercise judicial power. Litigants cannot be certain that the decisions in their cases are made without strategic considerations or inappropriate influences by the political branches affecting the votes of the justices if those justices lack permanent appointment. More importantly, the inferences from our analyses question the presumption that the judicial branch is capable of fulfilling the role many statesmen and scholars attribute to it. We assume that life-tenured justices are more insulated from external influences than those who lack it, but even the protections of Article III cannot ensure that sitting judges are entirely immune to being influenced by external pressures. Epstein and Knight (1998) describe several examples of circumstances in which the interests of the Court as a whole, or the justices collectively, arguably retreat from legal positions due to external pressure. They conclude that in these circumstances, justices are not averse to adjusting their decisions to reduce or avoid confrontation or threats to their institutional interests. We can more easily see the basis for justices' vulnerability to external influence in the admittedly rare recess appointment cases, but this is far from the only circumstance in which justices' interests are conditional on the favor of other actors.

Additional research on other recess appointees to lower federal courts is necessary to determine if other judges change voting pre- and post-confirmation. Unfortunately, we do not think it possible to combine that information with the analyses presented herein. Given the discretionary docket of the Supreme Court and other institutional factors that separate these justices from all other courts, the behavior of Supreme Court justices is unique among the federal judiciary. However, given the differences pre- and post-confirmation that we have discovered it is sobering to consider the implications that recess appointments cause for judicial independence.

Notes to Chapter 3

1. Holmes dissented in *Northern Securities v. United States* (1904) opposing the breaking up a railroad trust favored by the majority. The dissenting vote prompted Roosevelt's famous tirade of "I could carve out of a banana a judge with more backbone!" (Abraham 1999; Cushman 1996)

2. Senate Resolution 334.

3. 106 Cong. Rec. 12761 (1960); S. Rept. No. 1893, 86th Cong., 2nd Session 1-2 (1960).

4. The resolution was ultimately adopted by the Senate.

5. Testimony before Congress, 106 Cong. Rec. 18131 (1960).

Chapter Four

Appellate Court Recess Appointments and Voting
(With Pamela Corley)

Introduction

In this chapter, we examine the influence of recess appointments and judicial independence on appellate court judicial voting. We also explore this issue through the lens of separation of powers and judicial choice by studying appellate court judicial recess appointees who have later been confirmed by the Senate to full time Article III judicial positions. Following our analysis in Chapter Three, our strategy is to compare the votes of fourteen recess appointed judges of the U.S. Courts of Appeals during their temporary recess tenure with votes cast during a similar period immediately following Senate confirmation.

There are several reasons to address the recess behavior of Supreme Court justices and appellate court appointees separately. From nomination through confirmation, to the structures of the courts, docketing procedures, and voting practices, the United States Courts of Appeals and the Supreme Court are very different. First the Supreme Court is the only court explicitly created by Article III of the United States Constitution. All other courts, including the Courts of Appeals, are creations of Congress via statute. The outline for the appellate courts' present organization was not set in place until March 3, 1891, with the passage of the Everts Act, creating the Circuit Courts of Appeals. Congress changed the name to the Courts of Appeals with the Judicial Code of 1948. Initially, the Circuit Courts of Appeals were composed of nine regional courts, although the District of Columbia was added soon after in 1893. The Tenth Circuit was carved from the Eighth Circuit Court of Appeals by an Act of 1929, and in 1981 the Eleventh circuit was created by splitting the Fifth Circuit. In 1982 a specialized appellate court, the Federal Circuit, was created from the old Court of Claims and Court of Customs and Patents. As of 2006, there were 179 authorized courts of appeals judges.

The nomination process for appellate court judges is also quite different. Supreme Court nominations are handled by the White House, whereas lower court nominations must deal with the norm of Senate courtesy that is deference to the home state senator's interest in the nominee. While courtesy is not as important in the selection of Courts of Appeals nominees as it is for District Court nominees because Courts of Appeals cover several states, individual seats are usually identified with particular states, giving the home state senator some influence over the nomination (Giles, Hettinger, and Pepper 2001; Slotnick 2002).

The United States Supreme Court now has almost total control over its docket. For much of the twentieth century, the justices alone have chosen the cases they will hear and decide. This means that almost all of their votes are on significant cases and often on issues that are politically and ideologically polarized. In contrast the Courts of Appeal have mandatory dockets. Their cases frequently inspire little or no basis for legal or factual disagreement. In addition, the Supreme Court hears cases as a whole, whereas the vast majority of cases that Courts of Appeal judges hear are in rotating three judge panels. Rarely does an appellate court sit *en banc*.

The cultures of the Supreme Court and the Courts of Appeals are also quite different. Supreme Court justices are assumed to have no further ambition, having reached the top of the judicial hierarchy (Segal and Spaeth 1993). They usually work in isolation and there have been well-known instances of bitterness among the members. Justice McReynolds, for example, was well known to be anti-Semitic and refused to talk to Justice Brandeis and Justice Cardozo, the two Jewish members of the Supreme Court at that time (Pride 1996). McReynolds also made his disdain for Justice Stone well known. In contrast, the Courts of Appeals are known for their collegiality (Hettinger et al. 2006). This contributes further to the remarkable level of consensus and unanimity on these courts.

Thus, we offer separate comparisons of the recess and post-confirmation voting of judges on the U.S. Courts of Appeals in this chapter. Simply put, do these appellate court recess appointees vote differently during their temporary tenure than they do after securing Senate confirmation? Are the complaints of litigants and the fears of court observers that diminishing the constitutional protections of judges' independence compromises the exercise of judicial power justified?

Judicial Independence and Judicial Choice

Few would disagree that there is an element of strategic thinking in the vote choices of Article III Appellate Court justices. Even though a federal judge is given lifetime tenure, evidence demonstrates that the threat of congressional retaliation against the institution can constrain the choices of a judge (Cross and Nelson 2001, 1460-1473). A recess-appointed judge is in a far more precarious position. A recess appointee has no guarantee of lifetime tenure and confronts a very real threat of removal from the bench with the sitting of the next Congress.

The purpose of the Article III protections of judicial independence is clear—they ensure that the judicial branch is not subject to the inappropriate influence of other interests. As Hamilton explained in *Federalist* 78:

Periodical appointments, however regulated, or by whosoever made, would, in some way or other, be fatal to [the courts'] necessary independence. If the power of making them was committed either to the executive or legislature, there would be danger of an improper complaisance to the branch which possessed it; if to both, there would be an unwillingness to hazard the displeasure of either. (Rossiter 1961, 471)

The purpose of the Recess Appointment Clause is also clear—it allows the executive to keep the operations of government running even when the Senate is not in session and thus is unable to confirm presidential nominees, including judicial nominees. Along with the important value of judicial independence, the Recess Appointments Clause reflects the founders' commitment to continuity in government. Presidents now use the recess power even if Congress has a relatively brief intra-session break, however. As we have discussed, President George W. Bush appointed William Pryor to the Fifth Circuit Court of Appeals during a twelve-day mid-winter break by the Congress, while in the last days of his presidency Bill Clinton named Roger Gregory as the first African American on the Fourth Circuit Court of Appeals during a 20-day inter-session recess. It is a separation of powers game that pits the executive appointment power against the right of the Senate to offer advice and consent. The fact that Gregory, whose seat had gone unfilled for a decade despite several nominations over the entirety of the Clinton presidency, was eventually renominated by Clinton's opposite-party successor and confirmed by a Republican-controlled Senate demonstrates the subtle power of the status quo established by a recess appointment.

Judicial recess appointments, unlike those to executive positions, affect all three branches of government. While the recess clause can shift power over courts towards the president and away from Congress it can also affect the exercise of judicial power. If someone is placed on the court by recess appointment, that person might measure his decisions against the knowledge that the Senate Judiciary Committee could later question those rulings. Moreover, there is the argument that the Constitution guarantees litigants a hearing before judges enjoying the full protections of the Article III tenure and salary provisions.

The Supreme Court has recognized the importance of the Article III guarantees to the legitimate exercise of the judicial power of the United States. In *Northern Pipeline Co. v. Marathon Pipe Line Co.* (1982), the Court invalidated the Bankruptcy Act of 1978, concluding that Congress had impermissibly conferred judicial power onto courts that did not enjoy the protections of Article III. After subsequent revisions by Congress, bankruptcy judges serving fourteen-year terms can conduct proceedings, but their findings of fact and conclusions of law must be submitted to the district courts and both are subject to *de novo* review by Article III judges.

In addition, since recess appointees weaken the advice and consent role of the Senate, they arguably diminish the constitutional protections accorded to litigants. In short, a judicial recess appointment can damage judicial independence. Recess appointments to the executive branch of government generally do not pose this potential to undermine such a normatively important institution.

Judicial independence is an essential component of our legal system. Its goal is impartial, "law-based" decision making by judges, decisions made without regard for the political preferences of members of the other branches. "The judiciary," Gerald Rosenberg writes, "is independent to the extent its decision-making is free from domination by the preferences of elected officials" (1992, 371). Others define judicial independence as "a condition in which judges are entirely free from negative consequences for their decisions on the bench" (Baum 2003) or "the ability of the individual judge to make decisions based on the facts and the law without undue influence or interference" (Zemans 1999, 628).

Unpopular decisions have led to calls for greater political control over the judiciary in recent decades, leading to a debate over the proper balance between judicial independence and accountability. Not long ago, United States District Court Judge Harold Baer generated both a suggestion from the president that he consider resigning and a call for his impeachment from a presidential candidate when the judge granted a suppression motion. In response, Chief Judge John O. Newman of the Second Circuit Court of Appeals and three former chief judges issued a joint statement, asserting that "when a judge is threatened with a call for resignation or impeachment because of disagreement with a ruling, the entire process of orderly resolution of legal disputes is undermined" (Zemans 1999, 626).

In part, judicial independence is a function of institutional structure. The Constitution creates a federal judiciary as a separate and co-equal branch, a branch given the power of judicial review. Article III of the United States Constitution preserves the independence of judges in their decision-making process by guaranteeing a lifetime appointment and salaries that may not be diminished. In theory, this independence, plus the power of judicial review, allows the judiciary to "stand as the ultimate guardians of our fundamental rights" (Horsky 1958, 1111). Thus, judicial independence allows judges to uphold minority rights when they are under attack. The responsibility of the individual judge is to adhere to the definition of those rights as identified by the institutions of the judiciary. However, Ferejohn (1999) suggests that the independence of the judiciary is threatened if Congress and the president are ideologically unified and the judiciary is comprised of judges with a different ideology.

In the United States the other branches have control over jurisdiction, court creation, appointment, enforcement of court rulings, appropriations for the operation of the courts, and can impeach judges. Thus, there are many ways in which Congress and the president can exert influence over the federal judiciary. For example, Congress has adopted legislation restricting judicial review of habeas corpus petitions, sentencing guidelines that include mandatory minimums severely limiting judicial discretion, and the Civil Justice Reform Act of 1990 imposing oversight by district level committees and mandating alternative resolution programs (See Zemans 1999).

Thus, the process by which judges are appointed and retained can have an impact on judicial independence and accountability. When presidents and senators subject judicial nominees to ideological "litmus tests," they are routinely accused of undermining the nominees' independence, while the presidents and senators assert that asking about a nominee's "judicial philosophy" is a way to gauge whether the nominees are acceptable (See Geyh 2003).

Similar patterns exist for recess appointees. Jefferson B. Fordham, dean of the University of Pennsylvania Law School, remarked that a recess appointee "is serving under the overhang of Senate consideration of a nomination, which is not in harmony with the constitutional policy of judiciary independence" (106 Cong. Rec. 18131 (1960)). The Senate, of course, is not the only actor the recess-appointed judge might have to please. In a report written for the Congressional Research Service, Fisher (2005) observes that "(a) recess judge might also have to keep one eye out for the reaction of the White House, which would review decisions issued during the recess period to determine whether they justified nomination of the judge to a lifetime appointment." Such concerns led the House Judiciary Committee to issue a report in 1959 questioning the independence of judges sitting via recess appointment from political influence (Report 1959).

Herz (2005) employs an analogy to illustrate the difference between the situation of a judge sitting temporarily via recess appointment and that of a judge holding permanent commission. "These circumstances" he argues, "put the recess appointee in something of the same position as a law professor on a 'look-see visit'; his or her job becomes one extended interview. These circumstances are utterly at odds with the commitment to judicial independence reflected in Article III's good behavior clause and salary protections" (Herz 2005, 450).

While recess appointed judges will not have to confront the electorate, existing research on court nominations, judicial behavior, and judicial voting provides insight that buttresses the assertion noted above. Assuming that a recess appointee wants confirmation, the "electorate" that the nominee would care about most is the Senate. Research has shown that the median ideology of the Senate (Moraski and Shipan 1998) or even the partisan makeup of the Senate (Epstein and Segal 2005) can be critical to confirmation of the nominee as the president and Senate clash over the nominee each seeking an ideological advantage in the separation of powers struggles (Yates and Whitford 1998). The more liberal or Democratic the Senate the greater is the likelihood that the recess appointee would vote in a liberal direction.

Ideological voting is not the only way a recess-appointed justice could assuage Senate concerns. He would also likely avoid controversial rulings or behavior that would lead to unwanted attention. This could include avoiding separate opinion writing or making controversial votes, such as overturning precedent or state or federal law, or ruling against the state or federal government. Also, a judge may avoid liberal decisions dealing with high-profile issues that could mobilize political opposition, such as in cases dealing with civil liberties or rights claims.

Recent studies confirm some of these suspicions. For example, research on appellate court behavior shows that district court judges sitting by designation on the appellate court are less likely to issue separate opinions or otherwise engage in more dissensus oriented behavior (Hettinger, Lindquist, and Martinek 2006). In addition, a recess appointee might not want to alienate a senator by joining a decision to limit state or federal authority.

Hypotheses

Based on this we offer the following hypotheses regarding the differences of circuit court recess appointees' proclivity to vote in a liberal direction pre- and post-confirmation:

Hypothesis 1: A recess appointee will be less likely to cast liberal votes before Senate confirmation.

Hypothesis 2: A recess appointee will be more likely to vote in accordance with his ideology after Senate confirmation.

Hypothesis 3: A recess appointee will be more constrained by the judicial hierarchy after Senate confirmation.

3a: Controlling for the ideology of the judge, a recess appointee will be more likely to cast liberal votes as the relative liberalism of the median of the circuit within which he sits increases after Senate confirmation.

3b: Controlling for the ideology of the judge, a recess appointee will be more likely to cast liberal votes as the relative liberalism of the U.S. Supreme Court increases after Senate confirmation.

Hypothesis 4: A recess appointee will be more likely to depart ideologically from the president after Senate confirmation.

Hypothesis 5: A recess appointee will be more likely to cast liberal votes when the Senate is controlled by the Democrats before Senate confirmation.

Hypothesis 6: A recess appointee will be less likely to cast liberal votes in cases that are highly salient before Senate confirmation.

6a: A recess appointee will be less likely to cast liberal votes in cases that are subsequently petitioned for certiorari before Senate confirmation.

6b: A recess appointee will be less likely to cast liberal votes in cases when the court sits *en banc* before Senate confirmation.

Hypothesis 7: A recess appointee will be less likely to vote in a liberal direction on a case raising a civil liberties or rights issue before Senate confirmation.

Circuit Court Judges

The majority of judicial recess appointments have been to the Federal District courts. Historically this makes sense because the Federal District Court was created by the very first Judiciary Act of 1789 while the current structure of the Courts of Appeals did not come about until a century later. Of course, there are also many more district court seats than positions in the appellate courts, meaning more vacancies to fill. Table 4.1 presents a list of all recess appointed circuit court judges from 1900 through 2007.

One of the most striking details of the table is the length of the vacancies eventually filled by the "contemporary" recess appointments of Gregory, Pickering and Pryor in contrast to earlier instances. While weeks and months were adequate intervals to measure previous vacancies, the standard for these positions is years. The seat eventually filled by Gregory was vacant for over ten years, Pryor's for over three years and the seat to which Pickering was appointed went unoccupied for almost four and one-half years. Such conspicuous differences are indicative of the changes in tone and practice of judicial nomination and confirmation in the years between these appointments and the most recent previous recess appointment to the circuits in the first year of the Kennedy administration (Binder and Maltzman 2002, Holmes 2007).

Recess appointees to the federal circuit courts could hardly be characterized as marginal, undistinguished or uncontroversial appointments. Several of the judges listed in the table are considered outstanding jurists, with one, Thurgood Marshall, eventually becoming the first African American to serve on the United States Supreme Court. There are several other prominent judges among the recess appointees. David Bazelon, former chief judge of the United States Court of Appeals for the District of Columbia, received a recess appointment to his seat by President Harry Truman in 1949. Bazelon was the youngest judge ever appointed to that court and presided for seventeen years over what many consider

Table 4.1: Courts of Appeal Recess Nominees 1900 – 2008

Judge	President	Circuit	Appt. Date	Action	Vacant
Pryor, William H.	Bush II	11th	2/20/2004	Confirmed 5/6/2005	3 years, 2 months
Pickering, Charles	Bush II	5th	1/16/2004	Appointment expired 12/8/2004	4 years, 5 months
Gregory, Roger	Clinton	4th	12/27/2000	Conf. 7/20/2001	10 years, 8 months
Bell, Griffin B.	Kennedy	5th	10/5/1961	Conf. 2/5/1962	5 months
Gewin, Walter P.	Kennedy	5th	10/5/1961	Conf. 2/5/1962	4.5 months
Hays, Paul R.	Kennedy	2nd	10/5/1961	Conf. 3/16/1962	4.5 months
Marshall, Thurgood	Kennedy	2nd	10/5/1961	Conf. 9/11/1962	4.5 months
Boreman, Herbert	Eisenhower	4th	10/17/1958	Conf. 6/16/1959	7 months
Moore, Leonard P.	Eisenhower	2nd	9/6/1957	Conf. 2/25/1958	8 months
Schnackenberg, Elmer J.	Eisenhower	7th	11/17/1953	Conf. 2/9/1954	11 months
Hincks, Carroll C.	Eisenhower	2nd	10/3/1953	Conf. 2/9/1954	13 weeks
Danaher, John A.	Eisenhower	D.C. Cir.	10/1/1953	Conf. 3/30/1954	2 weeks
Hastie, William H.	Truman	3rd	10/21/1949	Conf. 7/19/1950	11 weeks
Swaim, Hardress	Truman	7th	10/21/1949	Conf. 2/8/1950	11 weeks
Washington, George T.	Truman	D.C. Cir.	10/21/1949	Conf. 4/28/1950	11 weeks
Dobie, Armistead	FDR	4th	12/19/1939	Conf. 2/1/1940	2 months
Kerner, Otto, Sr.	FDR	7th	11/21/1938	Conf. 2/1/1939	25 weeks
Thomas, Seth	FDR	8th	12/2/1935	Conf. 1/22/1936	2 days
Soper, Morris A.	Hoover	4th	5/6/1931	Conf. 1/12/1932	1 month
Hand, Augustus N.	Coolidge	2nd	5/19/1927	Conf.1/18/1928	1 month
Northcott, Elliott	Coolidge	4th	4/6/1927	Conf. 12/15/1927	11 days
Parker, John J.	Coolidge	4th	10/3/1925	Conf/ 12/14/1925	15 weeks
McCamant, Wallace	Coolidge	9th	5/25/1925	Appt exp.5/2/1926	None
Haight, Thomas G.	Wilson	3rd	4/1/1919	Conf. 6/24/1919	12 weeks
Alschuler, Samuel	Wilson	7th	8/16/1915	Conf. 1/16/1916	3 years, 10 months
Noyes, Walter C.	TR	2nd	9/18/1907	Conf. 12/10/1907	15.5 weeks
Ward, Henry G.	TR	2nd	5/18/1907	Conf. 12/17/1907	10 days
Buffington, Joseph	TR	3rd	9/25/1906	Conf. 12/11/1906	3 months
Adams, Elmer B.	TR	8th	5/20/1905	Conf. 12/12/1905	26 days

the nation's second most influential court (Berger 1993). Bazelon's decisions significantly expanded the rights of criminal defendants and laid the groundwork for the Supreme Court decision ordering President Richard Nixon to turn over White House tape recordings in the Watergate Scandal (Berger 1993).

William H. Hastie, a graduate of Amherst College and Harvard Law School, was the first African American to serve as a federal magistrate, the first African American to serve as governor of a federal territory (the Virgin Islands), and became the first African American on the United States Court of Appeals in 1949. The support of African American voters was crucial to President Truman's surprising 1948 re-election and he was pressured to appoint African Americans to federal judgeships by many supporters, including Mayor William O'Dwyer of New York (Goldman 1997, 99-100). Truman made this key appointment, along with 21 other judicial appointments including the first female district court judge, Burnita Matthews, during the 80th U.S. Senate's intersession recess. Hastie's subsequent confirmation met considerable opposition during lengthy, closed-door Judiciary Committee hearings conducted while the judge was hearing cases on the Third Circuit. The committee eventually returned the nomination favorably, although the committee chair did not release the final vote (Goldman 1997, 101).

Griffin Bell, a recess appointee of President John F. Kennedy to the Fifth Circuit, later became attorney general under President Jimmy Carter, was instrumental in vastly increasing the number of women and minorities to serve on the federal bench and in the Justice Department, and led the effort to pass the Foreign Intelligence Surveillance Act in 1978. Paul Hays, recess appointed to the 2nd Circuit on the same day as Thurgood Marshall, was a distinguished law professor, as was Armistead Dobie, a recess appointee to the 4th Circuit Court of Appeals. Dobie, while serving as dean, is credited with bringing the case study method of instruction to Virginia Law School (4th Circuit History 1998). Others had political careers prior to their appointment. For example, Otto Kerner, Sr. was the Illinois Attorney General and John Danaher was a former United States Senator from Connecticut.

Data, Model, and Analyses

Data

Our first step was to select a collection of votes for valid comparison. We gathered data on each of the judges' reported decisions from the date they arrived on the bench to the date they were confirmed by the Senate, decisions which could potentially have been affected by the temporary nature of their appointment. We also collected data for a similar number of case-votes from the same judges for the same amount of time following their confirmation. That is, if the judge sat as a recess appointee for one hundred days prior to confirmation, we gathered vote data from the date of the recess appointment to one hundred days following confirmation. Votes were considered "before" or "after" confirmation by comparing the report date of the case with the date of Senate confirmation. Certainly, some votes classified as post-confirmation by this rule were actually cast before the Senate vote, but because the conference dates are not known for these cases and judges are always free to change their votes up until the report date, any earlier demarcation would be arbitrary and possibly wrong. Furthermore, a judge casting a vote shortly before the Senate is scheduled to vote, knowing that the case would not be reported until afterward, could easily be free of whatever pressures he had felt when he knew that his votes could be scrutinized by the president or Senate before receiving a permanent commission.

Just as we did for our Supreme Court voting analyses, we rejected contrasting the justices' pre-confirmation behavior with the remainder of their careers on the bench. Changes in the institution of the Court, the dynamics of small-group decision-making, the political context, and the legal agenda facing the justices could all change, confounding recess effects. Furthermore, several studies indicate that many justices demonstrate ideological change over time on the bench, which manifests itself in behavioral changes (Epstein et al. 1998; Martin and Quinn 2002). Finally, many court scholars find that certain justices are prone to acclimation effects, changes in their behavior as they adjust to their new role and setting, although such periods of adjustment are thought to take a full term or two before noticeable differences appear (Hagle 1993; Hurwitz and Stefko 2004). This issue in particular cautions against casting too far from the recess period for comparable observations.

In the post-War era, sixteen judges have received recess appointments to the Appellate courts. For our purposes we modeled the votes of the fourteen appointees for whom we have voting data and ideological measures. They are David Bazelon, H. Nathan Swaim, David Fahy, George T. Washington, William H. Hastie, John A. Danaher, Carroll Hincks, Leonard P. Moore, Griffin Bell, Walter P. Gewin, Paul Hays, Thurgood Marshall, Roger L. Gregory, and William H. Pryor. The ideology metric used for this analysis, the Poole Basic or Common Space (1998), does not provide ideology scores for presidents before Eisenhower, but we extended our analysis back to the late 1940s by using Truman's Senate score for his ideology as president (Sala and Spriggs 2004). Elmer Schnackenberg and Walter Bastian were excluded because their short recess periods (84 and 73 days, respectively) did not produce any pre-confirmation votes. Charles Pickering, never confirmed by the Senate, could not be analyzed for the opposite reason.

The names, dates of appointment, dates of confirmation, and number of pre- and post-confirmation votes are all listed in Table 4.2. All of the recess appointed judges participated in fewer votes before confirmation than after, proba-

Table 4.2: Court of Appeals Recess Nominees Voting Data				
Judge	Recess Appt. Date	Confirmation Date	Votes during Recess Appt.	Votes following Recess Appt.
David Bazelon	10/21/1949	2/8/1950	10	15
H. Nathan Swaim	10/21/1949	2/8/1950	15	28
Charles Fahy	10/21/1949	4/4/1950	11	25
George T. Washington	10/21/1949	4/28/1950	17	17
William H. Hastie	10/21/1949	7/19/1950	35	46
John A. Danaher	10/1/1953	3/30/1954	7	31
Carroll Hincks	10/3/1953	2/9/1954	15	35
Leonard P. Moore	9/6/1957	2/25/1958	35	67
Griffin Bell	10/5/1961	2/5/1962	28	49
Walter P. Gewin	10/5/1961	2/5/1962	18	28
Paul Hays	10/5/1961	3/16/1962	44	22
Thurgood Marshall	10/5/1961	9/11/1962	85	104
Roger L. Gregory	12/27/2000	7/20/2001	11	29
William H. Pryor, Jr.	2/20/2004	6/9/2005	66	103

bly due to delay between taking the bench and their first reported cases. Having more post-confirmation votes increases the precision of estimates for the post-confirmation parameters and ensures that any votes cast pre-confirmation that are accidentally included among the post-confirm votes, if they are different, are overwhelmed by votes clearly cast after receiving life tenure.

In addition to the pre- and post-confirmation votes of the judges we collected data to test our hypotheses on the nature and direction of the voting. Specifically our dependent variable was the ideological direction of the vote. Following the coding scheme developed by Songer et al. for the United States Court of Appeals Database, we coded a vote as liberal (one) or conservative (zero). Votes which could not be classified as either conservative or liberal under the Songer rules were excluded from the analysis. We collected case-level data for several independent variables. For example whether or not a case was subsequently petitioned for certiorari review (one, zero otherwise), heard *en banc* (one, zero otherwise), whether the opinion was published (one, zero otherwise) and whether the case was a Civil Liberties/Civil Rights case (one, zero otherwise).

To test our ideological expectations, we collected ideology measures for relevant actors and institutions. The standard contemporary method of identifying political actors in the same ideological space, allowing cardinal distance comparisons, is the Basic or Common Space introduced by Poole (1998), extended to include federal lower court judges by Giles, Hettinger, and Peppers (2002) and to the U.S. Supreme Court by Epstein et al. (2007). We used these scores to place the president, home state senators, judicial circuits, and Supreme Court in comparable ideological space.

Placing the recess-appointed judges in that space proved a more difficult challenge. As noted above, Giles, Hettinger, and Peppers (2001, 2002) introduce a method for measuring the ideology of lower federal court judges that makes use of the norm of senatorial courtesy. Giles et al. (2002) attribute to lower federal court judges the ideology of the political actors involved in the judicial selection process. For judges selected under conditions when senatorial courtesy would apply, when the state in which the judge would sit has one or more senators of the president's party, they impute the ideology score, or the mean if more than one, of the relevant senator(s). If senatorial courtesy does not apply, the ideology score of the president is given to the judge. Although Giles et al. (2002) confirm the validity and performance of their measure for lower court judges generally, they do not investigate whether the scores are valid for judges selected under a heterodox method such as recess appointment. Are recess appointees selected under the same conditions as those who go through the conventional nomination and confirmation process without taking their seat beforehand?

Fortunately, another method is available to place recess appointees in the Common Space without relying on the selection process. Many scholars have attempted to place actors across institutions in shared ideological space with the use of "bridging observations," actors serving in both institutions. Poole (1998) for instance, uses instances of members of the House serving in the Senate and presidents serving in the House, Senate or both to create the comparable Common Space measures of members of Congress and presidents. Likewise, Nixon (2004) uses legislators with Common Space scores who served in administrative agencies to place Congress and agency appointees in comparable ideological space. Howard and Nixon (2003) exploit the fact that many members of Congress subsequently became federal court judges (sixty-three judges in all) to estimate a predictive model of first dimension Common Space scores using background characteristics of the judges (see also Howard 2007, 2008). This is the method that we employed to generate ideology scores for the recess-appointed Appeals court judges. The resulting scores correlate with the Judicial Common Space scores (those devised by the Giles et al. method) at 0.84, but several of the scores are considerably different, typically less extreme, than those imputed by the Giles et al. method.

With ideology scores for all relevant actors, we then calculated the ideological difference between each recess appointee and the median of the circuit within which he sat and the contemporaneous president and Supreme Court. The Common Space scores increase in conservatism—movement from negative to positive on the real line indicates increasingly conservative ideology—and the difference scores were calculated by subtracting the circuit, president, or Su-

Table 4.3: Descriptive Statistics—Pooled, Before, and After Confirmation						
Factor	Pooled		Before Confirmation		After Confirmation	
	Mean	Std. Dev.	Mean	Std. Dev.	Mean	Std. Dev.
Liberal Vote	0.456	0.498	0.488	0.501	0.434	0.496
Ideology of Judge (Conservatism)	-0.005	0.286	-0.028	0.289	0.001	0.284
Ideological Difference from Circuit Median	0.016	0.240	-0.001	0.232	0.026	0.243
Ideological Difference from Supreme Court	-0.032	0.327	-0.058	0.329	-0.013	0.325
Ideological Difference from President	0.119	0.214	0.126	0.202	0.114	0.220
Democratic Senate	0.737	0.441	0.752	0.432	0.724	0.447
Case petitioned for Certiorari	0.068	0.252	0.064	0.245	0.071	0.256
Case heard En Banc	0.052	0.223	0.067	0.250	0.043	0.204
Case concerned Civil Liberties or Rights Issue	0.359	0.480	0.307	0.462	0.391	0.488
	N = 996		N = 375		N = 621	

preme Court from the appointee's ideology. Thus, the differences measure how conservative the judge is relative to the actor in question.

We present descriptive statistics in Table 4.3.

As in the previous table, Table 4.3 splits the data into pre- and post-confirmation samples, but also shows the central tendency and variability for all of the observations combined. The proportion of liberal votes cast by these judges actually decreased slightly among the post-confirmation decisions, but the means and standard deviations of most other variables remained remarkably constant across periods. The only other notable difference was between the proportion of civil liberties and rights cases before and after confirmation.

Model: The outcome we are analyzing, the ideological direction of judges' votes, is dichotomous, thus we estimate logit models. The dependent variable, whether each recess appointed judge's vote in each case is liberal (one) or conservative (zero) is specified as a function of independent variables capturing the effect hypothesized above.

The first two variables in the model distinguish the pre-confirmation votes from the post-confirmation votes, the first coded one for cases reported during the judges' recess periods and zero afterward, the second with the opposite coding. Inclusion of both of these indicators, while suppressing the constant term, allows us to estimate separate intercepts for votes made pre-confirmation and post-confirmation.

Four variables are included making use of the Common Space ideology scores described above. The ideologies of recess appointees, estimated using the Howard and Nixon technique (2003) are entered directly. In addition, we also

Table 4.4: Hypotheses—Expected Directions of Effects on Voting Liberally

Factor	Expected Direction of Coefficients	
	Before Confirmation	After Confirmation
Underlying Propensities (Constants)	−	NA
Ideology of Judge (Conservatism)	NA	−
Ideological Difference from Circuit Median	NA	+
Ideological Difference from Supreme Court	NA	+
Ideological Difference from President	+	−
Democratic Senate	+	NA
Case petitioned for Certiorari	−	NA
Case heard *En Banc*	−	NA
Case concerned Civil Liberties or Rights Issue	−	NA
	N = 375	N = 621

include ideological differences of the judge's score from the median of the circuit in which the judge is sitting, the contemporaneous Supreme Court, and the contemporaneous president. We include a variable indicating whether (one) or not (zero) the Democratic Party controlled the Senate at the time of the judge's vote. The remaining variables are coded based on the cases themselves. In order to capture the salience of certain cases, their likelihood of being consequential enough to draw the attention of the president or Senate, we included indicator variables identifying cases that were petitioned to the Supreme Court after the Court of Appeals' decision, and whether the judge's vote was cast in an *en banc* hearing of a case. Although the certiorari petition follows the judge's vote, the presence or absence of such a petition is used as an indication of whether the litigants in the case were resourceful and sophisticated enough to pursue further appeals by seeking the attention of the highest court, something a judge might discern while casting the vote. The last variable captures cases that raise civil liberties or rights issues, the kind of cases that are more likely to raise controversies with political actors.

Table 4.4 restates our hypotheses in terms of the expected directions of the variable coefficients. For most variables, we specify directions for either the preconfirmation period post-confirmation. Conditions for which we expect no effect are indicated with NA.

Analyses

Our hypotheses propose that the effects of these factors will differ depending on whether or not the recess-appointed judge has been confirmed. Preconfirmation, we anticipate that recess-appointed judges will be less likely in general to vote liberally and even more so in cases subsequently appealed to the Supreme Court, heard *en banc*, or involving civil liberties or civil rights issues out of concern for stirring controversy about their impending nomination. We also expect that these judges will be conform to the preferences of those who must act on that nomination, being more likely to vote liberally when the Senate is controlled by Democrats and when the sitting president is more liberal than the judge. Following Senate confirmation, we hypothesize that more conservative judges will be less likely to vote liberally and that judges will be free of the constraint to conform to the ideology of the president. We expect that these judges will be constrained, however, by the preferences of their circuit and the U.S. Supreme Court, moderating their ideological predisposition in the direction of these hierarchical superiors.

In order to capture the conditional effects of these variables, we specify conditional models, estimating separate coefficients of the variables' effects before and after a judge is confirmed. We employ two strategies, a "multiplicative interaction" model, and a "regime" model. The former is the traditional "interactive" model widely used in social sciences in which variables whose effects on the outcome are thought to depend on the value of another variable are multiplied by that variable and the resulting term added to the specification. The unmultiplied terms are referred to as the "constituent" terms while the new terms are the "interactions." The second approach is useful when the condition upon which other effects are thought to depend is discrete, as it is here. We produce the "regime" model by multiplying the constituent terms by both variables indicating whether a vote was made before or after confirmation and enter those two sets of covariates into the model in place of the constituent terms. Thus, in the regime model, one set of covariates take their observed values for the before confirmation votes and are zero otherwise, while the other set take their observed values only after confirmation. The regime model allows us to estimate separate marginal effects on the outcome for the covariates across conditions (before and after confirmation) without the complications of the traditional interaction model (Brambor, Clark, and Golder 2006, 69).

As a basis for comparison, we estimated a logit model pooling the pre- and post-confirmation votes, allowing only the constant to vary across these conditions. The standard errors for this and the two subsequent models are heteroskedasticity-robust, clustered on the individual justices. The results appear in Table 4.5.

Coefficients and test statistics for the pooled model, combining votes cast before and after confirmation, appear in the first column. This model produces two statistically significant coefficients. Ideological difference from the circuit median has a positive effect and the presence of a civil liberties or civil rights issue has a negative impact on the likelihood of voting liberally. The ideology of the judge is controlled for separately, meaning that with ideology constant, the judges were more likely to cast a liberal vote when their circuit was more liberal than themselves (and less likely when the circuit was more conservative). This is consistent with the hypothesized effect for post-confirmation votes, which were by far the more numerous observations in the pooled data. The negative coeffi-

Table 4.5: Logit Models of Liberal Vote

Variables	Pooled Model	Interaction Model	Regime Model	
	β (Z)	β (Z)	β (Z)	$\beta_{Pre} \neq \beta_{Post}$ χ^2
Pre-Confirmation Intercept	0.123 (0.52)	-0.019 (-0.04)	-0.019 (-0.04)	
Ideology of Judge (Conservatism)	-1.481 (-1.27)	0.745 (0.36)	0.745 (0.36)	
Ideological Difference from Circuit Median	0.733** (2.09)	0.479 (0.58)	0.479 (0.58)	
Ideological Difference from Supreme Court	0.535 (0.48)	-1.460 (-0.79)	-1.460 (-0.79)	
Ideological Difference from President	-0.512 (-1.56)	-0.601 (-1.12)	-0.601 -1.12	
Democratic Senate	0.206 (0.91)	0.259 (0.46)	0.259 (0.46)	
Case petitioned for Certiorari	-0.461 (-1.71)	-1.283** (-2.35)	-1.283** (-2.35)	
Case heard *En Banc*	-0.126 (-0.52)	-0.078 (-0.17)	-0.078 (-0.17)	
Case concerned Civil Liberties or Rights Issue	-0.804*** (-7.37)	-0.480*** (-3.37)	-0.480*** (-3.37)	
Post-Confirmation Intercept	-0.019 (-0.10)	0.116 (0.68)	0.116 (0.68)	0.11
Ideology of Judge Post-Confirmation		-4.806** (-2.07)	-4.061*** (-2.76)	4.28**
Difference from Circuit Post-Confirmation		0.735 (0.69)	1.215** (2.34)	0.48
Difference from the Court Post-Confirmation		4.213** (2.25)	2.753** (2.10)	5.06**
Difference from President Post-Confirmation		-0.197 (-0.37)	-0.798** (-2.55)	0.14
Democratic Senate Post-Confirmation		-0.056 (-0.10)	0.203 (1.10)	0.01
Case petitioned for Cert Post-Confirmation		1.179** (2.35)	-0.104 (-0.38)	5.51**
Case heard *En Banc* Post-Confirmation		0.079 (0.13)	0.001 (0.00)	0.02
Civil Lib or Rights Issue Post-Confirmation		-0.544** (-2.12)	-1.034*** (-5.67)	4.49**
Akaike Information Criterion (AIC)	1321.904	1317.991	1317.991	

* $p < .10$; ** $p < .05$, *** $p < .01$, Two-tailed tests; SEs are heteroskedasticity-robust and clustered on judges N = 996

cient for civil liberties issues is consistent with the pre-confirmation hypothesis. The remaining coefficients are not statistically significant, but the pattern of their signs splits between the two sets of hypotheses. Of the four directional hypotheses specified for post-confirmation votes, all are in the expected direction, while four of the six directional hypotheses for pre-confirm votes are consistent with the results. The only coefficient with opposite expectations across regimes, ideological difference from the president, is consistent with the post-confirmation hypothesis.

The second column reports the results of the multiplicative interactive model. Looking first at the constituent terms, which can be interpreted as the marginal effects of these variables on vote choice for pre-confirmation votes, we find that two coefficients are statistically significant. Certiorari petition and civil liberties issues are significant and negative, consistent with the hypotheses for these variables. Of the remaining four directional hypotheses, three estimated effects are in the expected direction, all save ideological difference from the president, although none are statistically distinguishable from zero.

In this model, the interactive terms represent the departures from the estimated constituent effects for votes cast after confirmation, rather than marginal effects. Interpreting the estimated effects of changes in the variables on liberal voting requires taking account of both estimated effects, and assessment of whether those effects are statistically significant requires calculation of compound standard errors taking account of the covariance of the estimated effects. If anything, the coefficients and test statistics of interaction terms might reveal whether the marginal effects of the constituent terms are significantly conditional on each other, although perhaps not even that (Brambor et al. 2006, 74).

Comparing the interaction model to the pooled model, we find that for the estimated marginal effects of pre-confirmation votes, the significance of circuit difference disappears, the magnitude of its coefficient shrinking. Civil liberties issues remain statistically significant and negative, as expected. The coefficient for cases petitioned to the Supreme Court after review by the appeals judges, however, is now significant and negative, the coefficient substantially larger than in the pooled model. We hypothesized just such an effect.

The coefficients on those terms indicate the direction of the conditional effects on the constituent terms. Thus, we know that the effect of judges' ideologies on the likelihood of voting liberally departs changes after confirmation. This confirms our hypothesis for relationship was just as we expected—more conservative judges are less likely to cast liberal votes after confirmation, but not before. Ideological difference from the Supreme Court also changes, but in this case positively, suggesting that after confirmation judges are more likely to vote liberally as the Supreme Court's relative liberalism increases, holding the ideology of the judge and other conditions, constant.

Perhaps the most interesting of the interactive effects is the coefficient for cases petitioned for certiorari. The interactive term is positive, significant, and very similar in magnitude to the significant negative constituent term coefficient. This suggests that the impact of subsequent appeal to the Supreme Court mostly vanishes in the post-confirmation regime. Post-confirmation, a federal appeals judge is secure in their voting. The statistical significance of the overall effect is unknown, but since our expectation was that the certiorari effect would disappear after confirmation, learning that the resulting effect was not distinguishable from zero, which seems likely, would be consistent with our hypothesis.

The last remaining significant interaction is for the effect of civil liberties and rights issues after confirmation. The coefficient is in the same direction as the constituent term, suggesting that the impact of such issues makes liberal votes even less likely after the judges were confirmed. This is contrary to our hypothesis, which expected no effect after confirmation. The remaining coefficients are not significant, although the estimated effects are in expected directions. It remains to be seen whether the conditional marginal effects after confirmation are statistically significant.

Another issue with interactions, specific to nonlinear models such as logit, is that test statistics for the interactive terms in such models depend on the assumption that the residual variation in the dependent variable is equal across populations (Allison 1999). In other words, if the scale of the underlying propensities toward the outcome is different among pre-confirmation votes than among post-confirmation votes, that unequal residual variation could result in misleading hypothesis tests for interactive effects (Hoetker 2007). Fortunately, a class of models known as heterogeneous choice or location-scale models allows researchers to estimate valid test statistics even if residual variance differs across the populations defined by the interacting variable. We re-estimated the interactive and regime models using a heteroskedastic logit model, allowing the residual variance to change with the post-confirmation indicator, and confirmed that our results were robust to this assumption.

To untangle the marginal effects of the variables after confirmation, the regimes model results are reported in the third column of Table 4.5. Unlike the interaction model, in the regimes model effects estimated for the pre-confirmation votes are absent for the post-confirmation votes. Thus, the coefficients below the post-confirm intercept in column 3 are equivalent to the results of a logit model using only the post-confirmation votes. In fact, the results of the regimes model are equivalent to estimating two parallel logit models on the pre- and post-confirm votes separately. A virtue of estimating them together, however, is that we can easily test whether the pre-confirmation and post-confirmation coefficients are equal to each other. A series of chi-square tests are reported in the final column. Significant results indicate that we can reject the null that the two coefficients are equal.

The results for the pre-confirm votes are, as they should be, exactly the same as the constituent effects for the interaction model. The coefficients of the regime model for the post-confirm votes, however, are estimated effects of changes in these variables on liberal voting, rather than departures from the constituent effects. Interpreting these, we observe that the impact of judicial ideology on vote choice is negative after confirmation. The more conservative the judge, the less likely he is to cast a liberal vote, but only after Senate confirmation. These results are consistent with Hypothesis 2, and the chi-square test confirms that the coefficients are distinguishable from each other.

We find strong support for Hypothesis 3 which was that judges would be constrained by the judicial hierarchy after confirmation but not before, when their concerns were focused more on the political actors controlling their permanent appointment. This hypothesis has two parts: that liberal voting would be responsive to the Supreme Court and to the Court of Appeals circuit median only after the judge was confirmed. The coefficients for ideological difference from the high court and the circuit are not statistically distinct from zero for pre-confirmation votes, but significant and positive after confirmation, indicating that judges were more likely to vote liberally when the court within which they sit or the hierarchically superior court was more liberal, and less likely to cast liberal votes when they were more conservative. The Supreme Court coefficients are statistically distinct from each other as well, according to the chi-square test. The test for the circuit court effects does not confirm that the coefficients are different, but the fact that difference from the circuit was positive and significant in the pooled model, combined with the pattern for the pre- and post-confirm votes suggests that at the very least, the effect of circuit ideology is much more pronounced after permanent appointment.

The results for the ideology of the president are similar to those for the circuit courts. We estimate a statistically significant departure from the president's ideology only after confirmation. In that regime, the conservatism of the judge relative to the president makes liberal votes less likely, while the null cannot be rejected for votes before confirmation. Again, the chi-square test also fails to reject the null that the coefficients are similar, but ideological departure from the president appears to be much more muted before the judge is confirmed. We find no evidence that Democratic control of the Senate had any effect on liberal voting by recess appointees before or after confirmation. Thus, Hypothesis 5 receives no formal support from the results.

We do find support, however, for Hypothesis 6, which contended that judges would be reluctant to cast liberal votes on salient cases before they were confirmed. One of our indicators of case salience, the subsequent petition of a decision for review by the Supreme Court, has a significant and negative impact before confirmation on liberal voting, but a null finding afterward. The chi-square test confirms that these coefficients, both negative, are distinct, meaning that even if there is some negative effect of cert-petitioned cases after confirmation, it is considerably smaller than the effect before confirmation. We discover no effects of *en banc* cases on the incidence of liberal voting, either before or after confirmation, although the estimates have opposite signs and the pre-confirmation value is in the hypothesized direction, while the post-confirmation coefficient is essentially zero.

The results for our test of Hypothesis 7 are mixed. We expected that cases raising civil liberties and rights issues would be less likely to elicit liberal votes before confirmation but not afterward, but we found that civil liberties cases were less likely to receive liberal votes before and after confirmation. In fact, liberal votes were less likely in such cases after confirmation than before, as indicated by the relative sizes of the coefficients and the significant chi-square leads us to reject the null that these coefficients are equal.

We devised seven hypotheses about the differences in the effects of various ideological, political, and contextual effects on the propensity of recess-appointed judges to vote liberally before and after they received Senate confirmation. Many of those hypotheses were confirmed, some powerfully so. The most pronounced effect was the dramatic change in the relationship between ideology and vote choice before and after a judge is confirmed to a permanent judicial seat. Before confirmation, ideology has no discernable impact on votes and the coefficient estimate is contrary to its expected direction. After confirmation, however, the effect of ideology is substantially large, statistically significant, and in the direction predicted by decades of judicial politics scholarship. In short, judges' votes exhibit much more independence after confirmation than before.

Also consistent with our expectations, the judicial hierarchy does not have any statistically significant effect on the votes of judges sitting via recess appointment, but appears to constrain judges' vote choices after they are confirmed by the Senate. These results can be interpreted as the influences of the principle-agency relationships between appeals court judges, the circuits within which they sit, and the Supreme Court above them. Those influences are less pressing on the judges when the fate of their appointment is still in the hands of the president and Senate, but relevant after they gain the protections of Article III. Another even more troubling interpretation is that the "ideology" of the circuit and Supreme Court medians indicate the state of the law that the judges are bound to apply. These judges seem unaffected by such influences until they receive Senate confirmation. Recess appointees appear more inclined to follow their own legal lights, measured by their ideology, as well as to exhibit the influence of the legal system once they become permanent members of the judiciary.

We can learn more about the results graphically than through coefficients and test statistics. In Figure 4.1, we present predicted probabilities of the likelihood of voting liberally for pre- and post-confirmation recess appointees. In addition to confirmation, we also vary the salience factor, subsequent petition for certiorari. All other variables are set at central values, means for continuous variables and modes for dichotomous variables. The impact of case salience is quite clear. Typical cases that are not subsequently appealed to the Supreme Court are nearly 60 percent likely to receive liberal votes from our judges before confirmation, but varying only the certiorari variable reduces the predicted probability to below 30 percent. We observe that the statistically average case

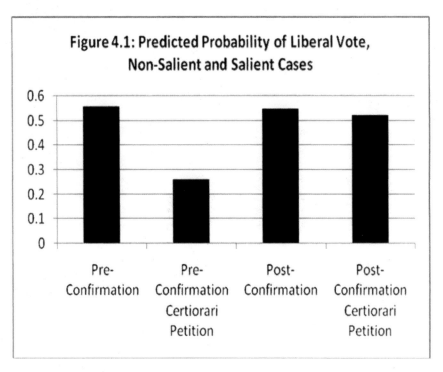

Figure 4.1: Predicted Probability of Liberal Vote, Non-Salient and Salient Cases

after confirmation has nearly the same likelihood of receiving a liberal vote as before, but varying the certiorari indicator has almost no effect on the likelihood of voting liberally. The impact of salience on vote choice before the Senate has confirmed the judge vanishes afterward.

In Figure 4.2, we graph changes in the predicted probabilities of a liberal vote across the range of judicial ideologies observed in our sample for judges pre-confirmation and post-confirmation. The X-axis indicates the conservatism of the judge, from left to right. All of the remaining variables are fixed at their central values, means for continuous variables and modes for binary variables.

For votes cast before confirmation, ideology has a mild but counterintuitive effect of increasing the likelihood of casting a vote. Following confirmation, however, the effect of ideology is pronounced and as expected. These appeals court judges are much more likely to cast liberal votes when they themselves are liberal after receiving Senate consent, and that probability falls sharply and consistently to the conservative extreme, ranging from about 90 percent for the most liberal judge to just above 10 percent for the most conservative.

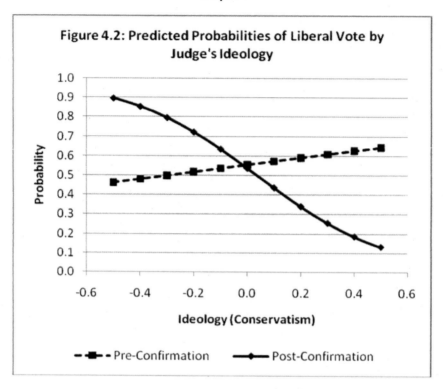

Figure 4.2: Predicted Probabilities of Liberal Vote by Judge's Ideology

Probability

Ideology (Conservatism)

- - ■ - - Pre-Confirmation   ——◆—— Post-Confirmation

Figure 4.3 presents a similar graph of the change in predicted probability of a liberal vote across the range of ideological difference between the judge and the median of his circuit. The measure is a difference, subtracting the median ideology from that of the judge, so positive numbers reflect how much more conservative the judge is than the circuit, while negative numbers indicate how much more conservative the circuit is than the judge. Our hypothesis for this variable was one of institutional constraint. We anticipated that after confirmation, judges would be more likely to cast liberal votes when the circuit was substantially more liberal than the judge, since the impact of the judge's ideology is accounted for separately. Alternatively, we expected that ideological difference from the circuit would have no effect before the judge becomes a permanent member of the judicial branch.

The predicted probabilities bear out these expectations. The effect of ideological difference from the circuit is nearly flat for pre-confirmation votes, but changes from below 40 percent to nearly 70 percent as the relative liberalism of the circuit grows. The effect of ideological difference after confirmation is about three times the effect before confirmation over the same range.

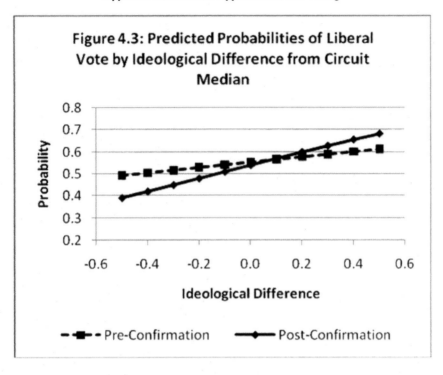

Figure 4.3: Predicted Probabilities of Liberal Vote by Ideological Difference from Circuit Median

Conclusions

The evidence indicates that judicial recess appointments do threaten judicial independence. Our results demonstrate that these judges did alter their voting pre-confirmation, based on their observed behavior afterward. Judges sitting by temporary recess appointment do not vote according to their ideological predispositions and do not appear to be responsive to the direction of their circuit or the Supreme Court. Rather, we contend, these judges are concerned with the impression that their actions on the bench make on the president who must renominate and support them and the Senate that must vote to confirm them. These judges also avoided liberal votes in cases subsequently appealed to the Supreme Court by the unsuccessful party and in cases raising civil liberties and civil rights issues during their recess appointment period.

In contrast, we found that these same judges' voting behavior was very consistent with their ideology, measured independently of their own voting records, after they were confirmed. Although many scholars might not see the virtue of judges voting consistently with their ideological predisposition, we see ideological voting at the appellate level as the exercise of individual discretion in cases based on sincerely held beliefs about the state of the law. Judges chosen by political actors to apply their understanding of the law to cases necessarily bring with them distinctions that are manifest in the exercise of judicial discretion. This exercise is entirely consistent with "good faith judging" in a way that voting in order to please actors outside of the judiciary is not (Gillman 2001).

We also find that the recess-appointed judges were much more responsive in their voting behavior to the ideological direction of the circuit in which they sat and the U.S. Supreme Court following their permanent appointment than they were beforehand. In a sense, judges sitting temporarily, awaiting the approval of the political branches to keep their jobs, are not full members of the judicial branch during that time, but visiting jurists on a "look-see" extended interview, as Herz (2005) characterizes the situation. The important distinction, however, between these situations is that their colleagues have no role at all in deciding whether the visiting judge will receive an offer of permanent employment.

Because recess appointees must still be confirmed by the Senate, they lack the independence accorded by the tenure and pay protections of Article III of the United States Constitution. Their exercise of judicial power, therefore, should be considered at least as suspect as the circumstance found unconstitutional in *Northern Pipeline Co.* (1982). Certainly the evidence presented herein demonstrates that judges sitting via recess appointment are not voting their sincere preferences. Judicial independence, along with judicial review, allows judges to fulfill their prescribed role of protecting minority rights when they are under attack, but a recess appointee must be mindful of the president and the Senate, strategically choosing to avoid controversial rulings and behavior that would lead to unwanted attention. Rather than acting as a member of an independent third branch with the protection of lifetime tenure, the recess appointee must keep "one eye over his shoulder on Congress."

Under a separated powers system, each branch has overlapping responsibilities and power subject to control and review by the other branches of government. However, once confirmed by the Senate, Article III judges are guaranteed lifetime tenure and protection from decreases in their salary. Although Congress does have some limited checks on the judiciary post-confirmation, and there is evidence that threat of congressional retaliation against the judiciary can constrain the choices of a judge, the evidence presented here shows that a recess appointee sits in a more precarious position, and, consequently, the independence provided by the Constitution is diminished.

Judges sitting via recess appointment are in a different position than confirmed justices. Our results raise serious concerns about the validity of permitting recess-appointed judges to exercise judicial power, but they also echo the concerns of scholars who question the presumption of judicial independence. We assume that life-tenured justices are more insulated from external influences, but even the protections of Article III cannot ensure that sitting judges are entirely immune to being influenced by external pressures.

Chapter Five

A Look at Modern Judicial Recess Appointments

Introduction

In this chapter, we focus on judicial recess appointments in the modern era. We noted in Chapter Two that the unavailability of data back to the beginning of the Republic make it impossible to include ideological distance measures between the president and Senate, public approval scores, and other useful factors in a study. The difficulty of disaggregating appointment data over such a lengthy period also limited our analysis. Closer study of judicial recess appointments confined to the modern era could take into account these additional factors and possibly find other ways in which the exercise of unilateral presidential power has been complicated since the institutionalization of the American presidency.

By focusing on modern appointments, we are able to use contemporary measures of ideology and determine how significant ideological compatibility between the president and Senate is to the recess appointment process. Similar to Chapter Two, we explore under what political and institutional circumstances a president is likely to make a judicial recess appointment and our analysis confirms much of what we learned in Chapter Two.

Earlier we noted significant differences in the use of judicial recess appointments between older and modern eras. In the early days of the Republic through the nineteenth century, president's used the judicial recess appointment power primarily for efficiency reasons. Poor communications and travel and long congressional recesses dictated the need for action by the executive to keep the operations of government going. The judiciary for much of the nineteenth century was severely hampered by shortages and this was especially acute as the size of the nation grew rapidly (Wheeler and Harrison 2005). Thus the use of the recess power to fill vacancies was a commonsensical and presumably non-controversial, non-strategic approach to governing.

In the modern era, judicial recess appointments are different and while conventional wisdom holds that a politically weak president is more likely to use the recess power to avoid the necessity of Senate approval, we again find to the contrary in the modern era. We argue that politically strong presidents are more likely than weaker presidents to make judicial recess appointments. Our ideological measures from this analysis support the conclusions from the partisan strength measures in the earlier chapter. In a Separation of Powers system the recess appointment power allows a president to move the judiciary ideologically closer to his preferences, but this opportunity carries risks that legislative support can relieve. To demonstrate this, we assess the literature on judicial appointments and judicial recess appointments. Next we offer a brief review of previous scholarship of presidential power. Then we present our data, methodology, and results of our study. Finally we offer our conclusions and suggestions for future research.

The Politics of Modern Appointments

For the current chapter, we designate the modern era a bit differently than in Chapter Two, wherein we dated it from the beginning of Franklin Delano Roosevelt's presidency. Here, we begin with the advent of the presidency of Harry S. Truman. We do so because only from this point forward do we have cardinal measures of ideology—the Common Space scores. Our dataset uses all appellate court judicial nominations from 1945 through 2006 and includes 17 recess appointees. We model the likelihood of a recess appointment measured as the time until a judicial vacancy is filled with a judicial recess appointment. In this manner, we show what factors lead to a decrease in time before a recess appointment and what circumstances lead to longer durations to a recess appointment.

As previously noted, recess appointments have become the focus of contention and negotiation between presidents and the Senate. Following several nonjudicial uses of the recess appointment by President Ronald Reagan, including one to the independent Federal Reserve Board of Governors, then-Senate Minority Leader Robert Byrd placed a hold on seventy other pending nominations, "touching virtually every area of the executive branch," according to the White House, as well as including federal judges (Fisher 2001, 11). Reagan's standoff with Byrd ended with the development of procedures for recess appointments, including notice prior to the beginning of the recess. Violation of this agreement became one of the issues surrounding President Clinton's controversial recess appointment of Roger Gregory to a seat on the 4th Circuit Court of Appeals. After the Democrats regained control of the Senate in the 1986 election, Senate Minority Leader Bob Dole (R-KS), a potential candidate for the presidency, raised the possibility of giving a recess appointment to Robert Bork in response to delay in Bork's confirmation hearings, a suggestion dismissed by a Senate Democrat as "playing politics" (Walsh 1987).

While there is a relationship to population growth and the expansion of the judiciary (Wheeler and Harrison 2005) scholars have begun to find that partisanship and partisan alignments can both trigger and deter needed growth of federal judicial positions (de Figueiredo et al. 2001; de Figueiredo and Tiller 1996). Judicial growth is much more likely under unified government (de Figueiredo and Tiller 1996) than under divided government. Politics and partisanship dominated decision to create judicial positions. Presidents and home state senators nominate judges to lower federal court positions because the nominee shares the party preferences of the nominating president and senator. If judicial expansion occurs it means that whoever is president will get to nominate several judges to lifetime positions and those judges are likely to have the same ideological preferences as the president.

For example, a bill with bipartisan sponsorship introduced in the Senate in 2008 calls for the creation of fifty additions to the Court of Appeals and District Courts (Leahy Senate press release 2008). Twelve new Courts of Appeals positions would be created and 38 Federal District Court judgeships will also come into being. Undoubtedly Senators Hatch and Leahy both sponsored the bill assuming that their preferred presidential candidate would win, thereby hoping to fill fifty conservative or fifty liberal positions.

Because of this, a Congress with one or more branches in control of the opposition party is far less likely to approve new judicial seats than under unified government. Conversely, a unified government will be far more inclined to create new judicial seats in order to achieve some ideological control over federal judicial rulings.

If Congress does create new judicial seats, then recess appointments can be particularly appealing to the president. As noted, a recess appointment to an Article III court allows the president to fill a vacancy with a favored candidate quickly, without the obstruction or rejection the confirmation process might produce. Such appointments are temporary, but an intrasession recess commission can last for nearly two years, if the recess falls early in the congressional session (Carrier 1994). This allows the president to appoint an ideologically compatible judge to serve on an Article III court producing rulings that the president favors for a significant period of time. Of course the president always has to be careful in the use of the recess appointment. As Gerhardt notes, "senators have invariably used their other powers, particularly oversight and appropriations, to put pressure on those choices" (2000, 174). Furthermore, the ability of a president to extend his influence beyond his terms of office by reshaping the federal judiciary through life-term appointments is not served, and may be frustrated, by the injudicious use of unilateral authority like the recess appointment power.

Strong presidents, those with strong partisan or ideologically compatible majorities in the Senate are well equipped to use the recess power and this power should also be used when there are new judicial seats to fill. Those are the presidents who can weather the controversy and potential harmful tactics of the Senate upset by intrusions on its institutional power and domain. Conversely weaker presidents would have to use such power sparingly and be more aware of intruding on Senate prerogatives. Thus a president with a Senate controlled by the opposition, or one with low approval or one in the fourth year of office, traditional measures of a constrained presidency (Segal, Timpone, and Howard 2000), might find it very difficult to justify or contemplate any sort of strategic use of the judicial recess power.

All of this leads us to believe that strong presidents and presidents with newly created, vacant judicial positions are going to be the most likely to use the recess power. In the next section we offer our data, models used and analysis.

Data, Model, and Analysis

Our interests lie in the likelihood of a specific appellate judicial vacancy being filled by a recess appointment and the political, institutional, and temporal factors affecting that likelihood. We restrict our present analysis to the post-war period for several reasons. First, although there had been circuit courts and appellate judges previously, the modern U.S. Circuit Courts of Appeals took shape only after the Act of 1891 drafted for that purpose. Also, our previous analysis indicates that the factors influencing use of recess appointments have different effects in the years before the onset of the "modern" presidency and afterward. Thus, any conclusions drawn from analyzing vacancies before the modern era may not be generalizable to the subsequent period. Accurate data on vacancies and appointments in the modern era are also considerably more accessible. Ideology scores for the president and the Senate and public approval data on the president's performance, of which we make use in our analysis, are only available for the modern era.

The term of the study for our analysis extends from the beginning of the Truman administration in 1945 to the end of the 109th Congress in the first days of 2007. During this period, seventeen judges were appointed by the president during Senate recesses to fill vacancies on the Circuit Courts of Appeals. We make use of the rich and extensive data available in the Multi-User Database on the Attributes of U.S. Appeals Court Judges, often referred to as the "Auburn" database. This database, as updated, provides background information about every judge serving on the courts of appeals from 1801 to 2000. For our purposes, the data also report characteristics of the seats and vacancies on the Circuit Courts of Appeal. We also coded data on Senate recesses and political control, much of it used in previous chapters, as well. Because our term of study is confined to recent decades, we can make use of the Basic Space preference scores described previously in Chapter Four that place federal government actors in ideological space comparable across institutions and time (Poole 1998). Thus, changes in the ideological distances between actors across time are reflective of genuine changes in relative ideological positions. Finally, we collected data on the collective yearly caseload of the circuit courts from reports of the Administrative Office of the Courts.

Several methods could be used to analyze presidents' decisions to fill existing judicial vacancies with recess appointees. We could treat each vacancy as an observation to be filled either by the conventional nomination and confirmation process or by recess appointment (Corley 2006). However, this approach neglects the effect that varying circumstances can have on the incidence of recess appointments. Conditions that make recess appointments unlikely at the time a vacancy is created could change as the vacancy persists. Another approach would be to follow the strategy used in chapter 2, examining the number of recess appointments made in a given year. This approach served well for our analysis of the full history of judicial appointments, but limiting our study to the modern era as we do in this chapter permits a more nuanced investigation of the qualities of individual vacancies and their effects on incidences of recess appointment.

The Event History Model

The approach we take accounts for both the incidence and timing of recess appointments to court of appeals vacancies. Our data disaggregates judicial vacancies to days vacant so that we can assess the impact of varying conditions on a president's decision to fill a judicial position during a Senate recess. We estimate an event history model, which considers the timing of events as well as their occurrence. Event history models are often referred to as "duration", "survival" or "hazard" models, depending on the interest of the researcher. Such models have been used in political science for some time now to study subjects as wide-ranging as policy diffusion (Berry and Berry 1990; Volden 2006), government duration (King, Alt, Burns, and Laver 1990; Strøm and Swindle 2002), democratization (Hannan and Carroll 1981; Lai and Melkonian-Hoover 2005), and international conflict (Bennett and Stam 1996; Regan 2002). Event history methods have been applied to various questions in judicial politics, including legal change (Benesh and Reddick 2002; Spriggs and Hansford 2002), judicial confirmation (Binder and Maltzman 2002; Shipan and Shannon 2003), and retirement (Zorn and Van Winkle 2000).

Applications of event history analysis typically model the "hazard rate" of a unit of analysis over a period of observation. The hazard rate can be conceived of as the "risk" or likelihood that a given unit of analysis experiences an event in a particular interval of time given that the event has not occurred at the beginning of that interval (Box-Steffensmeier and Jones 2004). We are interested in the risk that a judicial vacancy will be filled via recess appointment conditional on the fact that it has not previously been filled by Senate confirmation of a nominee. Event history analysis assumes that during the time intervals being studied, the units are "at risk" of experiencing the event. At the beginning of the observation period, a unit must be within the "risk set"—units eligible to experience the event—and when the event can no longer occur, the unit exits the risk set.

To conduct proper event history analysis of judicial recesses, we must structure our data in order to study judicial vacancies only when the likelihood of a judicial recess appointment taking place is greater than zero. The risk of a judicial recess appointment when the Senate is in session, for instance, is zero. Individual judicial vacancies also exit the risk set when the vacancy is filled otherwise. Thus, our data consist of every day in which a judicial vacancy existed and the Senate was in recess during our term of study from 1945 to 2007. The resulting dataset consists of 475 judicial vacancies observed over a total of 79,739 vacancy-recess days.

We model variation in the hazard rate from one vacancy-recess day to another as a function of covariates. Factors or conditions that we hypothesize will make recess appointments more likely will cause the hazard rate to increase, while factors or conditions that we expect to deter use of recess appointments will lead to a decline in the hazard rate. Our covariates reflect the hypotheses specified in the previous section. The independent variables in the duration model can be divided into characteristics of the Senate recesses, the judicial vacancies, and the political-institutional context of a given vacancy-recess day. They can also be characterized as a class of fairly constant circumstances or qualities and temporal qualities, or indicators of "political time."

Several covariates are qualities of the Senate recesses within which individual vacancy-recess days fall. We include a variable indicating whether a particular recess occurred intrasession. Another covariate measures the length of the instant recess. Finally, we coded a variable that measures the number of days from the vacancy-recess day in question to the end of the next congressional session, similar to the variable we used in Chapter Two as a measure of how long a temporary commission issued during the current recess would last. Because the unit of analysis for this model is the recess day, rather than the recess, this covariate decreases by one with every subsequent day within a Senate recess. The first two of these variables are comparatively constant qualities, while the third measures a particular, institutionally relevant understanding of time.

The next group of covariates for the duration model reflects features of the judicial vacancies, the actual units of our analysis. We code an indicator distinguishing judicial vacancies newly created by legislation from those that result from a judge vacating a previously existing seat. Another variable counts the length of the spell, or the number of recess days elapsed since the vacancy occurred. This variable serves to capture a form of "duration dependence," indicating how much time the Senate has spent in recess while the vacancy goes unfilled. Another form of time dependence is reflected in the next variable, which measures the number of days for each observation until Senate confirmation. For vacancies that are not filled by recess appointment, this is the number of days remaining until the vacancy is filled, but for seats filled by recess appointment, this quantity is the number of days until the vacancy is filled added to the number of days from the recess appointment to the day a nominee is confirmed permanently to the seat. The difference between the two measures the gain in days a recess appointee would be active on the bench over the conventional confirmation process. The first of these variables is constant across a vacancy spell, while the other two are, of course, time-varying.

The remaining variables capture political and institutional circumstances that are qualities of neither the Senate recesses or of the specific vacancies that constitute our data. The first of these is a measure of the executive activity of the president in office at the time. We use the same measure for this that we used in our complete history analysis in Chapter Two, the number of executive orders issued by the president during the current term. Although this quantity will change slowly, a number of vacancies span more than one presidential administration, even across different presidencies. We also include a measure of the public's approval of the president's performance in office, produced from the Gallup survey data made available by the Roper Center and transformed into a monthly series using the dyad ratios algorithm developed by James Stimson (1999). This algorithm produces a measure of the covariance of different series of data from survey marginals, recursively averaging ratios of different series of survey responses as indicators of the same underlying concept and placing the aggregate measures on a common metric.

Three more variables are included to capture conditions not specific to the vacancy or the recess. We coded a variable measuring the absolute distance between the Common Space ideology scores of the current president and the median of the Senate. This variable reflects the policy division between the president and Senate with more accuracy than the proportion of Senators of the president's party, given the heterogeneity of American political parties and especially the divisions over judicial nominations within parties that have arisen in decades past. The yearly circuit caseload variable, the number of appeals filed per year as reported by the Administrative Office of the Courts, is also included. Finally, the event history model has a time counter indicating the number of days from the beginning of our period of observation, roughly the beginning of the Truman administration. This variable measures the passage of time, rather than the duration of a spell or time until some point. Thus, it will capture any secular trend in the incidence of recess appointments over the course of the six decades of our study.

The Split Population Model

A complication of the event history approach is that standard models of this type assume that all observations in the dataset will eventually experience the event, even if the period of study does not last long enough to observe it. For our purposes, this means that every vacancy will eventually be filled by a recess appointment. Obviously, this is an unreasonable assumption. In fact, the duration of a judicial vacancy is a result of two processes, the conventional confirmation process and the president's choice to fill the seat via recess appointment. Either of these processes can end the vacancy. Failure to take into account the fact that most vacancies are not filled by recess appointment can introduce heterogeneity into the model and lead to incorrect estimates of the influence of the covariates on the phenomenon.

One way to address this problem is to model the observed duration as a result of two separate processes, the recess-vacancy duration and the exit of spells from the risk set by Senate confirmation. As constituted, the duration is equal to the number of days that the vacancy persists and the Senate is in recess. While the vacancy is potentially eligible to be filled by recess appointment on those days, it is not simultaneously at risk of being filled by confirmation on those days. Rather, confirmation ends the spell, but occurs during the "gap time" between recesses. Our solution is to model the observed duration to recess appointments conditional on the probability that the vacancy does not exit the risk set—is not filled—by confirmation before that day.

The "split-population" or "cure" model relaxes the assumption that all observations will eventually observe the event. The set of observations are a combination of two "populations": those that eventually experience the event and those which do not (these observations are referred to as "cured," reflecting the root of models such as this in biostatistics). The split-population model mixes the unconditional density of the hazard function with the probability that the unit is among the observations that will experience the event. This probability is typically estimated as a function of covariates using a standard dichotomous dependent variable model such as logit or probit.

Following this estimation strategy, we specify a split population duration model with the duration equation specified as above and a probit model predicting the likelihood that the vacancy will be filled by Senate confirmation without

Table 5.1: Descriptive Statistics

Variable	Mean	Std. Dev.	Minimum	Maximum
Intra-Session Recess	.659	.338	0	1
Judge-Days Gained by Recess Appointment	19.348	135.722	0	1377
New Seat	.217	.421	0	1
Length of Recess (days)	41.354	34.486	1	181
Recess-Vacancy Counter (days)	219.428	251.303	1	1630
Appointment Length (days)	232.959	131.040	0	694
Caseload	40,170.44	18,093.33	2,615	68,473
Presidential Approval	55.161	11.047	24.373	85.739
Executive Orders (thousands)	2.0483	.563	0.990	5.040
Ideological Distance of President from Senate Median	.479	.134	0.121	.677
Secular Time Counter (days)	15,979.22	4,722.12	0	22,406
Length of Vacancy (days)	1,008.616	848.560	1	3,692
Presidential Election Year	.272	.445	0	1
Divided President-Senate	.518	.500	0	1

N = 79,739

a recess appointment. The variables in this equation are the overall length of the vacancy in days, the indicator variable of whether the seat is a newly created vacancy, indicators of whether the vacancy is created in a presidential election year and whether the vacancy occurs during divided party control of the Senate and president, and the caseload variable. Descriptive statistics for our data are presented in Table 5.1.

Analysis

The results of the split-population event history model are reported in Table 5.2. The fully specified model improves the log-likelihood substantially over the null, which results in a very significant likelihood-ratio test and indicates a very good fit to the data. Considering the event history model first, we find many of our covariates to have statistically significant effects on the hazard rate. Positive coefficients reflect increases in the hazard rate, or a greater likelihood of observing a recess appointment, while negative coefficients indicate decreasing likelihood.

We find that intrasession recesses lead to a greater likelihood of a recess appointment in the modern era. Despite the widely held principle that appointments during the typically brief recesses taken within sessions of the Senate are disfavored and should be rare, presidents have been more likely to make such appointments since the end of World War II. This perhaps should not be surprising, since intrasession recesses can last considerably longer than those made after the *sine die* adjournment of the Senate. Intrasession recess appointments made shortly after the beginning of a session can last nearly two years, giving the appointee considerable time on the bench to conduct work and receive confirmation by the full Senate.

Consistent with this finding and our analysis from chapter 2, the length of time a recess commission would last is directly related to the likelihood of a recess appointment. The indicator variable for seats newly created by Congress approaches statistical significance and is positive. The counter of recess-vacancy days is positive and significant, indicating positive duration dependence. The more days the Senate spends in recess without acting on whatever nomination may be pending for a judicial vacancy, the greater the likelihood that the president will act to fill the vacancy unilaterally. Similarly, the difference in days between the confirmation date filling a vacancy permanently and the current day is positively related to recess appointments. Taking this quantity as an indication of the president's expectations of delay, this suggests that presidents are responsive to perceived gridlock.

Several of our results illustrate the complicated relationship between the president and the Senate with regard to recess appointments. Our finding from chapter 2, that "assertive" presidents as measured by the number of executive

Table 5.2: Split-Population Model of Days to Recess Appointment

Event History Analysis Variables	Time to Recess Appointment		
	Coefficient (SE)	Z-score	Marginal Effect
Intra-Session Recess	2.952**	2.70	19.142
	(1.093)		
Length of Recess (days)	0.00692	0.93	
	(0.00742)		
Appointment Length (days)	0.271***	5.39	1.027
	(0.00502)		
New Seat	1.709	1.84	
	(0.927)		
Recess-Vacancy Counter (days)	0.0128***	4.70	1.013
	(0.00272)		
Judge-Days Gained by Recess Appointment	0.00769***	6.76	1.008
	(0.00114)		
Executive Orders (thousands)	-3.031***	-4.64	0.0483
	(0.653)		
Ideological Distance of President from Senate Median	-7.038**	-2.57	0.000878
	(2.734)		
Presidential Approval	-0.0694*	-2.21	0.933
	(0.0313)		
Caseload	0.000221	1.74	
	(0.000127)		
Secular Time Counter (days)	-0.00204***	-5.14	0.998
	(0.000397)		
Constant	-14.092		

"Cure" Analysis Variables	Confirmation Prior to Recess Appointment		
	Coefficient (SE)	Z-score	Marginal Effect
Length of Vacancy (days)	0.0102*	2.02	-0.000163
	(0.00506)		
New Seat	-1.720*	-1.96	0.325
	(0.879)		
Presidential Election Year	1.994*	2.27	-0.0108
	(0.879)		
Divided President-Senate	0.636	0.83	
	(0.765)		
Caseload	-0.000747*	-2.04	0.0000144
	(0.000367)		
Constant	0.860		

Log-Likelihood	-34.699	LR Test (21): 252.11	
(Null = -137.451)		$p > \chi^2 = .000$	

* $p < .10$; ** $p < .05$, *** $p < .01$, Two-tailed tests; SEs are heteroskedasticity-robust
N = 475 Vacancies / 79,739 Vacancy-Days
Marginal Effects for event history analysis are instantaneous changes in the hazard rate; Marginal Effects for the cure analysis are average effects on the probability of observing a recess appointment.

orders issued are less likely to make recess appointments in the modern era. Judged by its marginal effect, this variable has a pronounced impact on the hazard, decreasing the hazard rate to 5 percent of its baseline value for every increase of one thousand executive orders. We also discover that the ideological distance of the president from the Senate median, a measure of the president's shared policy preferences with the chamber, is negatively related to recess appointments. This finding also supports conclusions drawn in chapter 2 that in the modern era Senate party strength is positively related to recess appointments. Contrary to the conventional wisdom that recess appointments are a tool primarily used by presidents without political support in the Senate, presidents with such support are more likely to use recess appointments to fill judicial seats. This suggests that it is minority obstruction, rather than majority opposition, that presidents are overcoming when they bypass the Senate confirmation process. Adding another dimension to this finding, we learn that presidential approval ratings of the public are negatively related to incidents of judicial recess appointment. Lastly, the secular time counter is negative, capturing the easily observable decline in recess appointments to the courts over our period of observation.

Turning our attention to the "cure" equation in the model, we observe that most of the variables in the specification are significant and in anticipated directions. The length of a vacancy is positively related to vacancies experiencing the "cure" of Senate confirmation. At least in the modern era, it appears, protracted vacancies are generally resolved not by unilateral action, but by eventual Senate action, despite recent high-profile counterexamples. Perhaps the most interesting finding in this set of covariates, newly created vacancies are substantially less likely to be terminated by Senate confirmation than those in pre-existing judicial seats. This finding suggests that for much of the modern era, judicial recess appointments are a collaborative endeavor between the Senate and the president, rather than a conflictual one. Bearing out conventional wisdom, the Senate is significantly less likely to fill vacancies during presidential election years than otherwise. Finally, we find that caseload significantly decreases the likelihood of a seat being filled by Senate confirmation. Caseload was positively related to recess appointment in the duration equation, but not significant. From this we might infer that as Hamilton suggested in the Federalist Papers, the executive is more responsive to concerns for the efficiency of government than is the legislature.

Conclusions

As noted in the beginning of this chapter, our findings here confirm much of our historical analysis from chapter 2. Here we focused solely on the modern presidents and their appointments and added measures of ideology and measures of judicial vacancy and whether or not legislation created new judicial positions.

We also included some additional measures of presidential strength and constraint. Our event history analysis finds that strong presidents are more likely to use the recess power than a constrained weak president. In addition, the creation of new judicial seats will lead to the use of the recess power.

Our results again suggest that contemporary use of the recess appointment power to fill federal judicial seats should be greeted with skepticism. modern presidents make recess appointments in an opportunistic fashion, combined with the legal and political controversy surrounding them, we believe that judicial recess appointments are unjustified. It also leads us to suggest that when resolutions are introduced to increase the size of the judiciary, however pressing the need, from a purely partisan and ideological viewpoint the opposition party is justified in viewing such legislation skeptically. The increase in the judiciary also means a greater likelihood of judicial recess appointment. That is especially so given the power position the president is likely to be in if such legislation passes Congress.

Chapter Six

A Skeptical View of Judicial Recess Appointments

The Decline and Fall of the Judicial Recess Appointment

The recess appointment had obvious value for much of United States governmental history. To late eighteenth century minds contemplating the formation and maintenance of the federal government there was a clear and precise need for the recess power. Travel was limited and inconsistent at best, illness a constant, and life spans short. A white male infant born in the United States in 1850 could expect to live to about thirty-eight, while a ten year old white male child in the same year could expect to live to forty-eight, having survived the perils of childhood illnesses. Of course, the average life expectancy decreases further if one adds minorities to the equation. By 2004 life expectancy in the United States had increased for men to over seventy-five years.

Of course, change has not been limited to lifespan. Transportation and travel, demands for federal services and bureaucratic and institutional growth have all accelerated over the course of United States constitutional history. Animals and wind powered the dominant modes of transportation in 1787 as distance travel required either a horse or sail. Even the steamboat was several years in the future. The federal government and federal judiciary were small even as compared to contemporary European standards and miniscule as compared to the present day. Congress, as we saw in Chapter Two took lengthy and extensive recesses and was in reality a part-time legislature. The early congresses took intersession recesses of up to two hundred and fifty days in length and it was not until the Nineteenth Congress that intersession recesses stabilized to fewer than twenty-five days per session.

To the eighteenth century framer the recess clause was necessary and proper. Sudden death or illness was a constant, travel uncertain and Congress often would be out of session. The operation of the federal government, however small and limited, needed to continue and the chief executive needed the recess appointment power. The president thus had the ability to fill up governmental vacancies, including judicial vacancy, at least until the end of the congressional session.

As we have seen, efficiency concerns throughout the nineteenth century significantly impacted the incidence of judicial recess appointments. Congressional recesses and the length of such recesses were positively related to judicial recess appointments. When intersession recesses and the length of recess declined, the incidence of the use of judicial recess appointments likewise declined.

However, as we have also seen, even as efficiency reasons decline, the obvious reason behind the Recess Appointment Clause, presidents continue to make judicial recess appointments. Instead it became a strategic game, one that is used not by weak presidents, constrained by Congress, but by active strong presidents, confident of confirmation, and anxious to push their choices into a judicial position so the appointee can begin to issue rulings in support of the president's policy positions. In addition, presidents are far more likely to make recess appointments early in the congressional session, ensuring months or even close to two years worth of rulings prior to the end of the appointment. In addition modern presidents are far more likely to make use of short "intrasession" recesses instead of the traditional, longer intersession recess to make the judicial recess appointment.

Many of these appointments have historical importance and most of the judges appointed during a recess were later confirmed, many enjoying long and distinguished careers. Thurgood Marshall, David Bazelon, William Hastie, Armistead Dobie, Griffin Bell, and William Hays were all appellate court recess appointees who went on to have distinguished judicial and legal careers. Hastie and Marshall's appointments broke down racial barriers and one can speculate that the recess appointments of these men helped break racial barriers by allowing them to demonstrate their fitness for office. A nomination under normal circumstances might have induced sufficient opposition to prevent either from ever holding office.

Prominent Supreme Court justices were also appointed through the recess process. Fifteen Supreme Court nominees began their career through a recess appointment. Again several distinguished jurists took office through this power, including Oliver Wendell Holmes, Jr. and the first Justice John Harlan. In the modern era, President Eisenhower made use of the recess appointment power to seat Earl Warren, William Brennan, and Potter Stewart. Warren and Brennan in particular were extremely influential in the development the civil liberties and civil rights revolution.

However, as we have also seen, these nominees do not vote the same way before and after confirmation. While we do not have sufficient data to make firm conclusions on the modern Supreme Court justices, the evidence does show a difference in voting behavior. As shown in Chapter Three, Warren and Stewart voted differently during the time they sat as recess appointees, taking into account the partisan make-up of the Senate. In addition, Brennan and Stewart were less likely to cast a controversial vote pre-confirmation, and both Warren and Brennan were more likely to write discretionary opinions post-confirmation.

Our evidence for appellate court appointees was far more conclusive. In Chapter Four we demonstrate that recess-appointed judges did alter their voting pre-confirmation, based on their observed behavior afterward. Judges sitting by temporary recess appointment did not vote according to their ideological predispositions and did not appear to be responsive to the direction of their circuit or the Supreme Court. Rather, we contend, these judges are concerned with the impression that their actions on the bench make on the president who must renominate and support them and the Senate that must vote to confirm them. These judges also avoided liberal votes in cases subsequently appealed to the Supreme Court by the unsuccessful party and in cases raising civil liberties and civil rights issues during their recess appointment period.

In contrast, we found that these same judges' voting behavior was very consistent with their ideology. We also found that the recess-appointed judges were much more responsive in their voting behavior to the ideological direction of the circuit in which they sat and the U.S. Supreme Court following their permanent appointment than they were beforehand. In a sense, judges sitting temporarily, awaiting the approval of the political branches to keep their jobs, are not full members of the judicial branch during that time, but visiting jurists on a "look-see" extended interview.

Finally our look at modern era recess appointees in chapter 5 with the full use of ideological as well as partisan controls confirms much of what we found in chapter 2's historical overview. Modern strong, active presidents strategically use the recess appointment power to install judicial nominees "ahead of the curve" thereby ensuring a faithful nominee carrying out the policy preferences of the appointing president. In this chapter we found that an intrasession, as opposed to the longer more formal intersession, recess was *more* likely to lead to a judicial recess appointment. In addition, new seats and greater value of the recess appointment as measured by the length of time a commission would last increased the likelihood of a judicial recess appointment. In addition, presidents in the fourth year of office are found to be more likely to make a judicial recess appointment, reflecting the difficulty of getting the Senate to confirm an appointee in such circumstances. However, just as we found in chapter 2, a strong president is more likely to make use of the recess power than a weak president. In chapter 2 presidents with strong Senate majorities in the modern era were more likely to appoint a judicial recess nominee. In this later analysis we use ideological distance as the reference point. Here as the ideological distance between the president and Senate increases, the president is less likely to make a recess appointment.

In this case subsequent confirmation becomes tenuous and thus the value of the appointment itself lessens because the president might not have the benefit of the confirmed judge voting in sync with presidential preferences. In fact the cost of the recess appointment could mean the loss of presidential capital and good will for other projects and proposals. Thus with limited presidential resources and significant constraints a president with policy preferences at great distance from the Senate simply cannot afford the slight benefit offered by the judicial recess appointment.

The perhaps unintended irony of this process and modern strategic use of the recess appointed power is the lack of efficacy of the appointment, at least from the policy preferences point of view of the president. As our analyses show, there is considerable doubt that the recess appointee during the time of the recess actually provides the appointing president with any great policy benefit. Judicial recess appointees simply do not appear to vote their sincere policy preferences. The voting is quite constrained and mostly non-ideological. While one might argue that this forces the appointee to apply the facts and the law instead of substituting an ideological preference, it also means that the recess appointee is not voting in accord with the president who appointed him or her, at least until full Senate confirmation. Simply put, a conservative or liberal president who recess appoints a conservative or liberal judge will not have the benefit of ideologically conservative rulings unless and until the appointee is confirmed by the Senate.

Whither the Judicial Recess Appointment Power

This of course begs the question of the purpose or reason for continuing the use or threat of the use of the judicial recess appointment power. Before discussing this we recognize that any proposal to change or eliminate the recess appointment power would have to be in the form of a constitutional amendment. That would require two-thirds of each house of Congress to vote in favor of an amendment and approval of three-fourths of the states. Constitutional amendments are rare events, perhaps rightly so. Many scholars have noted the problems with various parts of the Constitution (Eskridge, Jr. and Levinson 1998) and such analyses are worthwhile in promoting necessary debate over constitutional reform, even if the proposals never result in the introduction of a congressional resolution.

Given our findings in the book, we would like to enter our small contribution to this ongoing debate. It is time to consider, at least for the judiciary, the need for the judicial recess appointment power. As efficiency justifications have declined over the past two centuries, so too have judicial recess appointments. In the age of a full time Congress, longer and healthier lives, rapid travel, and instantaneous communication, there is little compelling reason for the recess appointment power, at least for judicial appointments. Since we have not studied other presidential recess appointments, we remain neutral as to that question.

Some might argue that given extreme Senate delays of nominations the president needs the flexibility to use the recess power to keep the operations of the federal judiciary going. Judicial appointments have not kept pace with population growth and partisan wrangling over judges and judicial ideology has prevented the courts from attending to civil and criminal matters even though most of these cases raise little or no ideological controversy. The facts and law of the vast majority of cases coming before the lower courts are clear, and the decisions unanimous. One conservative law professor argued that given Senate obstruction and the ongoing War on Terror, vacant judicial positions endanger the nation by preventing the courts from issuing critical rulings and opinions on important legislative and national security matters (Williams 2002).

Even if one does not agree that the War on Terror is imperiled, there is some merit to this position on judicial business. The three most recent recess appointees, Roger Gregory, Charles Pickering, and William Pryor, were appointed to offices that had been vacant for more than ten, three, and four years respectively. These delays contrast dramatically with recess appointments of the twentieth century, where vacancies were measured in days, weeks, or at most months rather than years. Thus there are very real differences between the nineteenth and the twenty-first centuries. However, there are still arguments to be made in favor of the recess appointment power on efficiency grounds. Combustion engines have replaced horse power, but partisanship affects judicial appointment politics profoundly, and the nation suffers from a lack of seated judges. Hence, one could claim that there is, especially in times of national emergency, a pressing need for the president to use the recess appointment power to appoint federal judges.

However, this sentiment ignores both political reality and remains an unproven empirical assertion. Empirically unmet judicial positions due to partisan wrangling has now occurred at least over several presidencies, yet those efficiency reasons are neither the reasons cited by the nominating presidents for the recess appointments, nor do these new efficiency reasons seem to be supported by our data and analyses. Modern presidents think and use the recess appointment power in a strategic ideological fashion. Efficiency concerns even in an age of a "global war on terror" are secondary if though of at all.

Perhaps more importantly are the judicial independence concerns. Whatever one thinks about judicial rulings, whether one agrees with former Attorney General Edwin Meese's now famous assertion that ". . . it seems fair to conclude that far too many opinions are policy choices [rather] than articulations of constitutional principle" (1986), judicial independence is bedrock of the federal judicial system. Whether it is for the protection of minority rights or viewpoints or freedom from oversight by the electoral majority and elected officials, in our system the third branch enjoys virtually complete independence from presidential and congressional interference.

For better or worse, that leaves federal judges free to vote their preferences or use some standard or the facts and the law or some combination of all three as guidelines for voting and opinions. However, recess appointees do not have that freedom and the data and analysis shows that they do not vote their preferences and thus do not enjoy the same freedom as the other judges in our system.

This means that the potential for a ruling from a recess-appointed judge and a judge confirmed by the Senate can be very different, and certainly this was not contemplated by the framers when they set the parameters for Article III judges and at the same time allowed the president to appoint judges through the recess power.

It is this confirmed limitation on judicial independence that is the most troubling aspect of the modern use of the recess power. The voting behavior of the recess judge differs markedly from the confirmed appointee. Justice varies by the type of judge and that is not tolerable.

Thus as efficiency justifications have diminished to practical nonexistence and as we learn of the differences in voting behavior one can make a strong argument that the recess appointment power, at least as it pertains to the judiciary, is no longer necessary. Of course, that would require a constitutional amendment and we have already noted the difficulty, if not impossibility of such an amendment. The fate of recess appointments rests with the political branches.

Our theory and results predicts that a president with a strong partisan majority in the Senate and one who also enjoys ideological compatibility with the Senate is more likely to make use of the recess appointment power. Thus if such a political situation emerges over the next several years the possibility exists for greater use of the recess power. Divided government has prevented this for many years. However, our theory and results also predict that the voting record of the recess appointee might vary significantly during the recess period from the preferences of the president. Thus a strong president might use the power, but the president might be very disappointed with the results.

References

"Fourth Circuit History: Remembering the Fourth Circuit Judges: A History from 1941 to 1998." 1998. *Washington & Lee Law Review* 55: 471-526 (1998).

Abraham, Henry J. 1992. *Justices and Presidents: A Political History of Appointments to the Supreme Court*, 3rd. Edition. New York Oxford: Oxford University Press.

Abraham, Henry. 1999. *Justices, Presidents, and Senators: A History of the U.S. Supreme Court Appointments from Washington to Clinton*. Rowman and Littlefield: Lanaham, Md.

Allison, Paul D. 1999. "Comparing Logit and Probit Coefficients across Groups." *Sociological Methods & Research* 28(2): 186-208.

Alvarez, R. Michael, and John Brehm. 1995. "American Ambivalence Towards Abortion Policy: Development of a Hetreoskedastic Probit Model of Competing Values." *American Journal of Political Science* 39(4): 1055-89.

Baum, Lawrence. 2003. "Judicial Elections and Judicial Independence: The Voter's Perspective." *Ohio State Law Journal* 64:13.

Becker, Theodore L. 1970. *Comparative Judicial Politics: The Political Functionings of Courts*, New York: Rand McNally.

Bell, Lauren Cohen. 2002. "Senatorial Discourtesy: The Senate's Use of Delay to Shape the Federal Judiciary." *Political Research Quarterly* 55: 589-608.

Benesh, Sara C., and Malia Reddick. 2002. "Overruled: An Event History Analysis of Lower Court Reaction to Supreme Court Alteration of Precedent." *The Journal of Politics* 64(2): 534-550.

Bennett, D. Scott, and Allan Stam. 1996. "The Duration of Interstate Wars, 1816-1985." *American Political Science Review* 90: 239-257.

Berger, Marilyn. 1993. "David Bazelon Dies at 83; Jurist Had Wide Influence." *New York Times.* http://query.nytimes.com/gst/fullpage.html?res= 9F0CE6DA143DF932A15751C0A965958260. February 21.

Binder, Sarah, and Forrest Maltzman. 2002. "Senatorial Delay in Confirming Federal Judges, 1947-1998." *American Journal of Political Science* 46: 190-199.

Brace, Paul, and Melinda Gann Hall. 1995. "Studying Courts Comparatively: The View from the American States." *Political Research Quarterly* 48: 5-29.

Brace, Paul, and Melinda Gann Hall. 1997. "The Interplay of Preferences, Case Facts, Context, and Structure in the Politics of Judicial Choice." *Journal of Politics* 59: 1206-1231.

References

Brambor, Thomas, William Clark, and Matt Golder. 2006. "Understanding Interaction Models: Improving Empirical Analyses." *Political Analysis* 14(1): 63-82.

Buck, Stuart, James C. Ho, Brett H. McGurk, Tara Ross, and Kannon K. Shanmugam. 2004. "Judicial Recess Appointments: A Survey of the Arguments." Federalist Society Paper.

Burbank, Stephen B., and Barry Friedman. 2002. *Judicial Independence at the Crossroads: An Interdisciplinary Approach.* Thousand Oaks, CA: Sage Publications, Inc.

Cameron, A. Colin, and Pravin K. Triveldi. 1998. *Regression Analysis of Count Data.* New York: Cambridge University Press.

Cardozo Law School Symposium. 2005." Jurocracy and Distrust: Reconsidering the Federal Judicial Appointments Process" Cardozo Law School Conference reprinted in *Cardozo Law Review* 26(2): 579.

Carrier, Michael A. 1994. "When Is the Senate in Recess for Purposes of the Recess Appointments Clause?" *Michigan Law Review* 92: 2204.

Chow, Gregory C. 1960. "Tests of Equality Between Sets of Coefficients in Two Linear Regressions." *Econometrica* 28:591-605.

Cooper, Philip J. 2002. *By Order of the President: The Use & Abuse of Executive Direct Action.* Lawrence, KS: University Press of Kansas.

Corley, Pamela C. 2003. "Recess Appointments to Independent Agencies, 1977-2000: Necessity or Strategy?" Paper presented at the annual meeting of the Midwest Political Science Association, Chicago, Illinois.

Corley, Pamela. 2006. "Avoiding Advice and Consent: Recess Appointments and Presidential Power." *Presidential Studies Quarterly* 36(4): 670-680.

Cross, Frank B., and Blake J. Nelson. 2001. "Strategic Institutional Effects on Supreme Court Decisionmaking." *Northwestern University Law Review* 95: 1437-1493.

Cushman, Claire, ed. 1996. *The Supreme Court Justices: Illustrated Biographies.* Washington DC: CQ Press.

Curtis, Thomas A. 1984. "Recess Appointments to Article III Courts: The Use of Historical Practice in Constitutional Interpretation." *Columbia Law Review* 84: 1758.

Deering, Christopher J., and Forrest Maltzman. 1999. "The Politics of Executive Orders: Legislative Constraints on Presidential Power." *Political Research Quarterly* 52:767-783.

de Figueiredo, John M., Gerald Gryski, Emerson H. Tiller, and Gary Zuk. 2000. "Congress and the Political Expansion of the United States District Courts." Unpublished Manuscript SSRN.

de Figueiredo, John M., and Emerson H. Tiller. 1996. "Congressional Control of the Courts: A Theoretical and Empirical Analysis of Expansion of the Federal Judiciary," *Journal of Law and Economics* 39: 435-462.

Epstein, Lee, and Jack Knight. 1998. *The Choices Justices Make*, Washington, DC: CQ Press.

Epstein, Lee, and Jeffrey A. Segal. 2000. "Measuring Issue Salience." *American Journal of Political Science* 44: 66-83.

Epstein, Lee, and Jeffrey A. Segal. 2005. *Advice and Consent: The Politics of Judicial Appointments*. Oxford: Oxford University Press.

Epstein, Lee, Jeffrey A. Segal, Harold J. Spaeth, Thomas G. Walker. 2007. *The Supreme Court Compendium: Data, Decisions & Developments*. Washington, DC: CQ Press.

Epstein, Lee, Andrew D. Martin, Jeffrey A. Segal, and Chad Westerland. 2007. "The Judicial Common Space." *Journal of Law, Economics, & Organization* 23: 303-325.

Eskridge, William. 1991. "Reneging on History? Playing the Court/ Congress/President Civil Rights Game." 79 *California Law Review* 613.

Eskridge, William, and Sanford Levinson, eds. 1998. *Constitutional Stupidities: Constitutional Tragedies*. New York: New York University Press.

Ferejohn, John. 1999. "Independent Judges, Dependent Judiciary: Explaining Judicial Independence." *Southern California Law Review* 72: 353-384.

Ferejohn, John, and Charles Shipan. 1990. "Congressional Influence on Bureaucracy." *Journal of Law, Economics, and Organization* 6: 1-20.

Fisher, Louis. 2001. CRS Report for Congress. "Recess Appointments of Federal Judges."

Fisher, Louis. 2005. "Federal Recess Judges." U.S. Congressional Research Service Report for Congress. Library of Congress.

Gerhardt, Michael J. 2000. *The Federal Appointment Process*. Durham, NC: Duke University Press.

Geyh, Charles Gardner. 2003. "Judicial Independence, Judicial Accountability, and the Role of Constitutional Norms in Congressional Regulation of the Courts." *Indiana Law Journal* 78: 153-221.

Giles, Micheal W., Virgina A. Hettinger, and Todd C. Peppers. 2002. "Measuring the Preferences of Federal Judges: Alternatives to Party of the Appointing President." Emory University Typescript.

Giles, Micheal W., Virgina A. Hettinger, and Todd Peppers. 2001. "Picking ederal Judges: A Note on Policy and Partisan Selection Agendas." *Political Research Quarterly* 54:623–641.

Goldman, Sheldon. 1997. *Picking Federal Judges*. New Haven CT: Yale University Press.

Hagle, Timothy M. 1993. "Freshman Effects' for Supreme Court Justices." *American Journal of Political Science*, 37: 1142-1157.

Hall, Melinda Gann. 1987. "Constituent Influence in State Supreme Courts: Conceptual Notes and a Case Study." *Journal of Politics* 49: 1117-1124.

References

Hall, Melinda Gann 1992. "Electoral Politics and Strategic Voting in State Supreme Courts." Journal *of Politics* 54: 427-446.

Hannan, Michael T., and Glenn R. Carroll. 1981. "Dynamics of Formal Political Structure: An Event-History Analysis." *American Sociological Review* 46: 19-35.

Harrison, Marion Edwyn. 2003. "Comparing Two Federal Court Recess Appointments." *Accuracy in Media Online.* January 30. http://www.aim .org/publications/guest_columns/harrison/2004/jan30.html.

Hartnett, Edward A. 2005. "Recess Appointments of Article III Judges: Three Constitutional Questions." *Cardozo Law Review* 26: 377.

Herz, Michael. 2005. "Abandoning Recess Appointments?: A Comment on Hartnett (and Others)." *Cardozo Law Review* 26: 443-461, p. 450.

Hettinger, Virginia A., Stefanie Lindquist, and Wendy L. Martinek. 2006. *Judging On a Collegial Court: Influences on Federal Appellate Decision Making.* Charlottesville, VA: University of Virginia Press 2006.

Hoetker, Glenn. 2007. "The Use of Logit and Probit Models in Strategic Management Research: Critical Issues." *Strategic Management Journal.* 28(4): 331-343.

Holmes, Lisa M. 2007. "Presidential Strategy in the Judicial Appointment Process." *American Politics Research* 35: 567-594.

Horsky, Charles A. 1958. "Law Day: Some Reflections on Current Proposals to Curtail the Supreme Court." 42 *Minnesota Law Review* 42: 1105.

Howard, J. Woodward 1968. "On the Fluidity of Judicial Choice." *American Political Science Review* 62: 43-56.

Howard, Robert M., and David C. Nixon. 2003. "Local Control of the Bureaucracy: Federal Appeals Courts, Ideology, and the Internal Revenue Service." *Washington University Journal of Law & Policy* 13: 233-256.

Howard, Robert M., and Henry F. Carey, Jr. 2004. "Courts and Political Freedom: A Measure of Judicial Independence" *Judicature* 87(6): 285-290.

Howard, Robert M. 2007. "Controlling Forum Choice and Controlling Policy: Congress, Courts, and the IRS." *Policy Studies Journal* 35(1): 109-123.

Howard, Robert M. 2008. "Courts, Justice, and Governing Coalitions and the Audits of Low-Income Taxpayers" *Journal of Theoretical Politics* 20(2): 181-200.

Hurt, Charles. 2004. "Bush again installs a judge at recess; Defies filibuster of Democrats." *The Washington Times.* p. A01, February 21.

Hurwitz, Mark S., and Joseph V. Stefko. 2004. "Acclimation and Attitudes: 'Newcomer' Justices and Precedent Conformance on the Supreme Court." *Political Research Quarterly* 57: 121–129.

Johnson, Timothy, and Andrew M. Martin. 1998. "The Public's Conditional Response to Supreme Court Decisions." *American Political Science Review* 92: 299.

References

Johnston, David. 2007. "Messenger in Prosecutors' Firings Quit." *New York Times*, Section A, p. 14, March 6.

Judicial Independence. *Southern California Law Review* 72: 353-384.

King, Gary. 1986. "How Not to Lie with Statistics: Avoiding Common Mistakes in Quantitative Political Science." *American Journal of Political Science* 30: 666-687.

King, Gary, and Lynn Ragsdale. 1988. *The Elusive Executive: Discovering Statistical Patterns in the Presidency*. Washington, DC: CQ Press.

King, Gary, James E. Alt, Nancy E. Burns, and Michael Laver. 1990. "A Unified Model of Cabinet Dissolution in Parliamentary Democracies." *American Journal of Political Science*. 34(3):846-871.

Krause, George A., and David B. Cohen. 1997. "Presidential Use of Executive Orders, 1953-1994." *American Politics Quarterly* 25:458-481.

Krause, George A., and Jeffrey E. Cohen. 2000. "Opportunity, Constraints, and the Development of the Institutional Presidency: The Issuance of Executive Orders, 1939-96." *Journal of Politics* 62:88-114.

Lai, Brian, and Ruth Melkonian-Hoover. 2005. "Democratic Progress and Regress: The Effect of Parties on the Transitions of States to and Away from Democracy." *Political Research Quarterly*. 58(4): 551-564.

Lewis, David E., and James Michael Strine. 1996. "What Time is It? The Use of Power in Four Different Types of Presidential Time." *Journal of Politics* 58: 682-706.

Lewis, Neil A. 2004. "Bypassing Senate for Second Time, Bush Seats Judge." *The New York Times*, p. 1, February 21.

Light, Paul C. 1982. *The President's Agenda: Domestic Policy Choice From Kennedy to Carter*. Baltimore: Johns Hopkins University Press.

Marshall, Bryan W., and Richard L. Pacelle, Jr. 2005. "Revisiting the Two Presidencies: The Strategic Use of Executive Orders." *American Politics Research* 33:81-105.

Martin, Andrew, and Kevin Quinn. 2002. "Dynamic Ideal Point Estimation Via Markov Chain Monte Carlo for the U.S. Supreme Court 1953-1999." *Political Analysis* 10: 134-153.

Martinek, Wendy, Mark Kemper, and Steven R. Van Winkle. 2002. "To Advise and Consent: The Senate and Lower Federal Court Nominations, 1977-1998." *Journal of Politics* 64: 337-361.

Massie, Tajuana D., Thomas G. Hansford, and Donald R. Songer. 2004. "The Timing of Presidential Nominations to the Lower Federal Courts." *Political Research Quarterly* 57: 145-154.

Mayer, Kenneth R. 1999. "Executive Orders and Presidential Power." *Journal of Politics*. 61: 445-466.

Mayton, William Ty. 2004. "Recess Appointments and an Independent Judiciary." *Constitutional Commentary* 20: 515-555.

References

McCarty, Nolan, and Rose Razaghian. 1999. "Advice and Consent: Senate Responses to Executive Branch Nominations 1885-1996." *American Journal of Political Science* 43: 1122-1143.

Meese III, Edwin. 1986. Speech Before the American Bar Association. *The Great Debate*. Washington, DC: The Federalist Society, pp. 31-42.

Moraski, Bryan, and Charles R. Shipan. 1999. "The Politics of Supreme Court Nominations: A Theory of Institutional Constraints and Choices." *American Journal of Political Science*. 43: 1069-1095.

Nixon, David C. 2004. "Separation of Powers and Appointee Ideology." *Journal of Law, Economics, and Organization* 20 (2):438-57.

Nixon, David C., and David L. Goss. 2001. "Confirmation Delay for Vacancies on the Circuit Courts of Appeals." *American Politics Review* 29: 246-274.

Note, "Recess Appointments to the Supreme Court—Constitutional but Unwise?" 10 Stan. L. Rev. 10: 124, 140 (1957).

Pederson, William D., and Norman W. Provizer (eds.). 2003. *Leaders of the Pack: Polls & Case Studies of Great Supreme Court Justices*. New York: Peter Lang Publishing.

Poole, Keith T. 1998. "Estimating a Basic Space From a Set of Issue Scales." *American Journal of Political Science* 42:954–993.

Pyser, Steven M. 2006. "Recess Appointments To The Federal Judiciary: An Unconstitutional Transformation Of Senate Advice and Consent." *University of Pennsylvania Journal of Constitutional Law* 8:61 – 133.

Ramseyer J.M., and E.B. Rasmusen. 1997. "Judicial Independence in a Civil Law Regime: The Evidence from Japan." *Journal of Law, Economics, and Organization* 13: 259-286.

Ramseyer, J.M. 1994. "The puzzling (in)dependence of courts: A comparative approach." *Journal of Legal Studies* 23: 721-747.

Regan, Patrick M. 2002. "Understanding Civil War: Third-Party Interventions and the Duration of Intrastate Conflicts." *The Journal of Conflict Resolution* 46(1): 55-73.

Report. 1959. "Recess Appointments of Federal Judges." House Committee of the Judiciary, 86th Cong. 1st Sess.

Rosenberg, Gerald N. 1992. "Judicial Independence and the Reality of Political Power." *The Review of Politics*. 54: 369-398.

Rossiter, Clinton, ed. 1961. *The Federalist Papers: Alexander Hamilton, James Madison, and John Jay*. New York: Mentor.

Sala, Brian R., and James F. Spriggs II. 2004. "Designing Tests of the Supreme Court and the Separation of Powers." *Political Research Quarterly* 57: 197-208.

Salzberger, E., and P. Fenn. 1999. "Judicial independence: Some evidence from the English Court of Appeals." *Journal of Law and Economics* 42: 831-847.

References

Segal, Jeffrey A., and Harold J. Spaeth. 1993. *The Supreme Court and the Attitudinal Model*. New York: Cambridge.

Segal, Jeffrey A., Richard C. Timpone, and Robert M. Howard. 2000. "Buyer Beware? Presidential Influence Through Supreme Court Appointments." *Political Research Quarterly* 53: 557-573.

Segal, Jeffrey A., and Harold J. Spaeth. 2002. *The Supreme Court and Attitudinal Model* Cambridge: Cambridge University Press.

Shipan, Charles R., and Megan L. Shannon. 2003. "Delaying Justice(s): A Duration Analysis of Supreme Court Confirmations." *American Journal of Political Science*. 47(4): 654-668.

Shull, Steven A. 1997. *Presidential-Congressional Relations: Policy and Time Approaches*. Ann Arbor: University of Michigan Press.

Silverstein, Gordon. 2007. "The Warren Court and Congress" in *Earl Warren and the Warren Court: The Legacy in American and Foreign Law*. ed. by Harry Scheiber. Lanham, MD: Lexington Books.

Skowronek, Stephen. 1993. *The Politics Presidents Make: Leadership from John Adams to George Bush*. Cambridge: Harvard University Press.

Slotnick, Elliot E. 2002. "A Historical Perspective on Federal Judicial Selection." *Judicature* 86 (July-Aug): 13-16.

Songer, Donald. R. "The United States Courts Of Appeals Data Base." *The Review of Politics* 54(3): 369-398.

Strøm, Kaare, and Stephen M. Swindle. 2002. "Strategic Parliamentary Dissolution." *American Political. Science Review* 96(3): 575-91.

United States Senate Press Release. 2008. "Leahy, Hatch, Feinstein, Schumer Introduce Bill to Increase Federal Judgeships and Help Reduce Judicial Backlogs." http://leahy.senate.gov/press/200803/031308c.html. March 13.

Van Natta, Jr., Don. 1996. "Judges Defend a Colleague from Attacks." *New York Times*. March 29, http://query.nytimes.com/gst/fullpage.html?res=9D06EFDA1539F93AA15750C0A960958260

Vanberg, Georg. 2001. "Legislative-Judicial Relations: A Game-Theoretic Approach to Constitutional Review" *American Journal of Political Science* 45: 346-361.

Walsh, Edward. 1987. "Reagan's Power to Make Recess Appointment is Noted," *The Washington Post*, p. A8, July 28.

Wheeler, Russell R., and Cynthia Harrison. 2005. "Creating the Federal Judicial System." 3rd. ed. *Federal Judicial Center*.

Whittington, Keith E., and Daniel P. Carpenter. 2003. "Executive Power in American Institutional Development." *Perspectives on Politics* 1:495-513.

Wigton, Robert C. 1996. "Recent Presidential Experience with Executive Orders." *Presidential Studies Quarterly*, 26:473-484.

References

Williams, Richard. 2006. "OGLM: Stata module to estimate Ordinal General-
ized Linear Models." http://econpapers.repec.org/software/bocbocode/
s453402.htm.

Williams, Victor. 2002. "Why President Bush Should Use Recess Appointments
to Fill Wartime Vacancies." Findlaw.com. January 1.

Yalof, David A. 1999. *Pursuit of Justices: Presidential Politics and the Selection of Supreme Court Nominees*. Chicago: University of Chicago
Press.

Yates, Jeff, and Andrew Whitford. 1998. "Presidential Power and the United
States Supreme Court." *Political Research Quarterly* 51(2): 539-550.

Zemans, Frances Kahn 1999, "The Accountable Judge: Guardian of Judicial
Independence." *Southern California Law Review* 72: 625-655. p. 628.

Cases Cited

Barenblatt v. United States, 360 U.S. 109 (1959).

Ex Parte McCardle, 74 U.S. (7 Wall.) 506 (1869).

Ex Parte Milligan, 71 US (4 Wall.) 2 (1866).

Northern Pipeline Co. v. Marathon Pipe Line Co., 458 U.S. 50 (1982).

United States v. Woodley, 726 F.2d 1328 (9th Cir. 1982).

Watkins v. United States, 354 U.S. 178 (1957).

Index

111

constitutional stupidities, 9
Coolidge, Calvin, 5, 15, 64
Corley, Pamela C., 8, 18, 57, 87
Cross, Frank B., 58
Curtis, Benjamin R., 36
Curtis, Thomas A., 31, 36
Cushman, Claire, 56

Danaher, John A., 64, 65, 66, 67
Davis, David, 36
de Figueiredo, John M., 84
Deering, Christopher J., 18
Dobie, Armistead, 64, 65, 96
Dole, Bob, 16, 84
Driscoll, Alfred, 41

Edmondson, J.L., 1, 2
Eisenhower, Dwight, 3, 5, 15, 16,
    17, 35, 36, 41, 42, 44, 45, 55,
    64, 66, 96
Epstein, Lee, 12, 13, 34, 35, 40, 44,
    45, 56, 61, 66, 67
Eskridge, William, 34, 98
Evans v. Stephens, 1, 5, 14
Everts Act, 57
Ex parte McCardle, 35
Ex parte Milligan, 35

Fahy, David, 66, 67
Federalist Papers, 2, 93
Federalist No. 78, 59
Federalist Society for Law and
    Public Policy, 23
Fenn, P., 39
Ferejohn, John, 34, 37, 60
Fillmore, Millard, 15
Fisher, Louis, 16, 31, 36, 61, 84

Ford, Gerald, 15
Fordham, Jefferson B., 39, 61
Foreign Intelligence Surveillance
    Act, 65
framers, 2, 4, 5, 7, 12, 34, 100

Garfield, James A., 15
Gerhardt, Michael J., 19, 85
Gewin, Walter P., 64, 66, 67
Geyh, Charles Gardner, 39, 61
Giles, Michael W., 58, 67, 68
Gillman, H., 80
Golder, Matt, 48, 71
Goldman, Sheldon, 12, 65
Grant, Ulysses S., 15
Great Depression, 21, 42
Gregory, Roger, 4, 12, 14, 16, 30,
    59, 64, 66, 67, 84, 99

Hagle, Timothy M., 44, 66
Haight, Thomas, 64
Hall, Melinda Gann, 39
Hamilton, Alexander, 2, 11, 58, 93
Hand, Augustus, 64
Hannan, Michael T., 87
Hansford, Thomas G., 13, 87
Harding, Warren J., 15
Harlan, John, 35, 36, 96
Harrison, Benjamin, 15
Harrison, Cynthia, 83, 84
Harrison, Marion Edwyn, 4
Harrison, William Henry, 15, 16,
    35
Hart, Henry, 3, 5
Hastie, William H., 64, 65, 66, 67,
    96
Hatch, Orrin, 85
Hayes, Rutherford B., 15
Hays, Paul, 64, 65, 66, 67

Whittington, Keith E., 18
Williams, Richard, 47
Williams, Victor, 4, 99
Wilson, Charles R., 2
Wilson, Woodrow, 15, 64
Woodbury, Levi, 36
Woodley, Janet, 2, 38

Yalof, David A., 12

Yates, Jeff, 13, 40, 61
York, Byron, 4

Zemans, Frances Kahn, 37, 39, 60, 61
Zero-Inflation Equation, 24, 25, 26, 28, 29, 31
Zorn, Chris, 44, 87